CRIMINAL MACABRE ™

a cal mcdonald mystery™

To F. W. Murnau

CRIMINAL MACABRE™

a cal mcdonald mystery™

TWO RED EYES

Story by **Steve Niles**

Interior art by **Kyle Hotz**

Colors by **Michelle Madsen**

Letters by **Nate Piekos for Blambot!**

Cover art by **Tim Bradstreet**

Dark Horse Books®

Editor **Shawna Gore**

Assistant Editor **Jemiah Jefferson**

Designer **Amy Arendts**

Publisher **Mike Richardson**

This book collects issues 1-4 of Criminal Macabre: Two Red Eyes, published by Dark Horse Comics.

Published by Dark Horse Books,
A division of Dark Horse Comics, Inc.
10956 SE Main Street
Milwaukie, OR 97222

September 2007
First edition
ISBN-10: 1-59307-843-9
ISBN-13: 978-1-59307-843-0

1 3 5 7 9 10 8 6 4 2

Printed in China

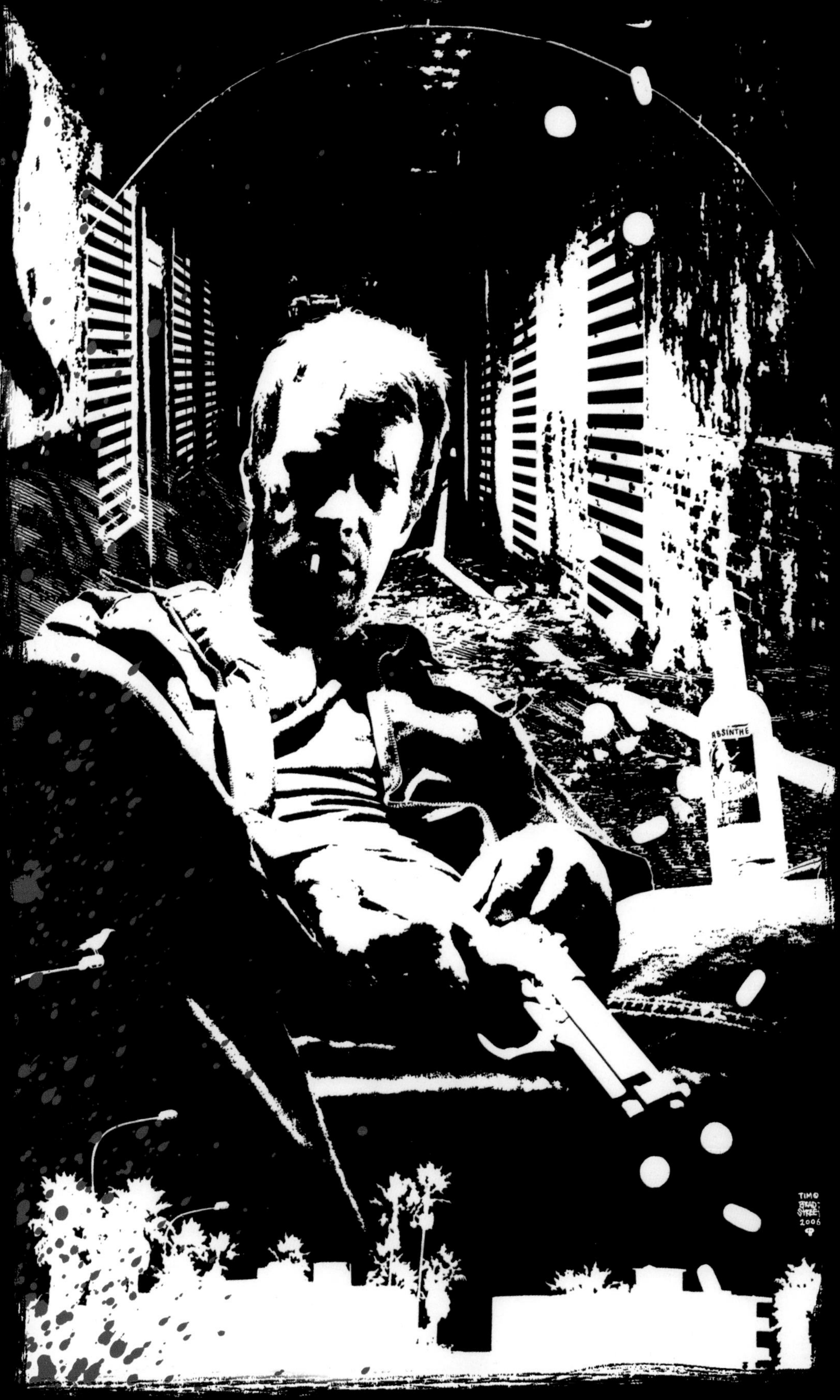
ABSINTHE
TIM
BRAD-
STREET
2006

CHAPTER ONE

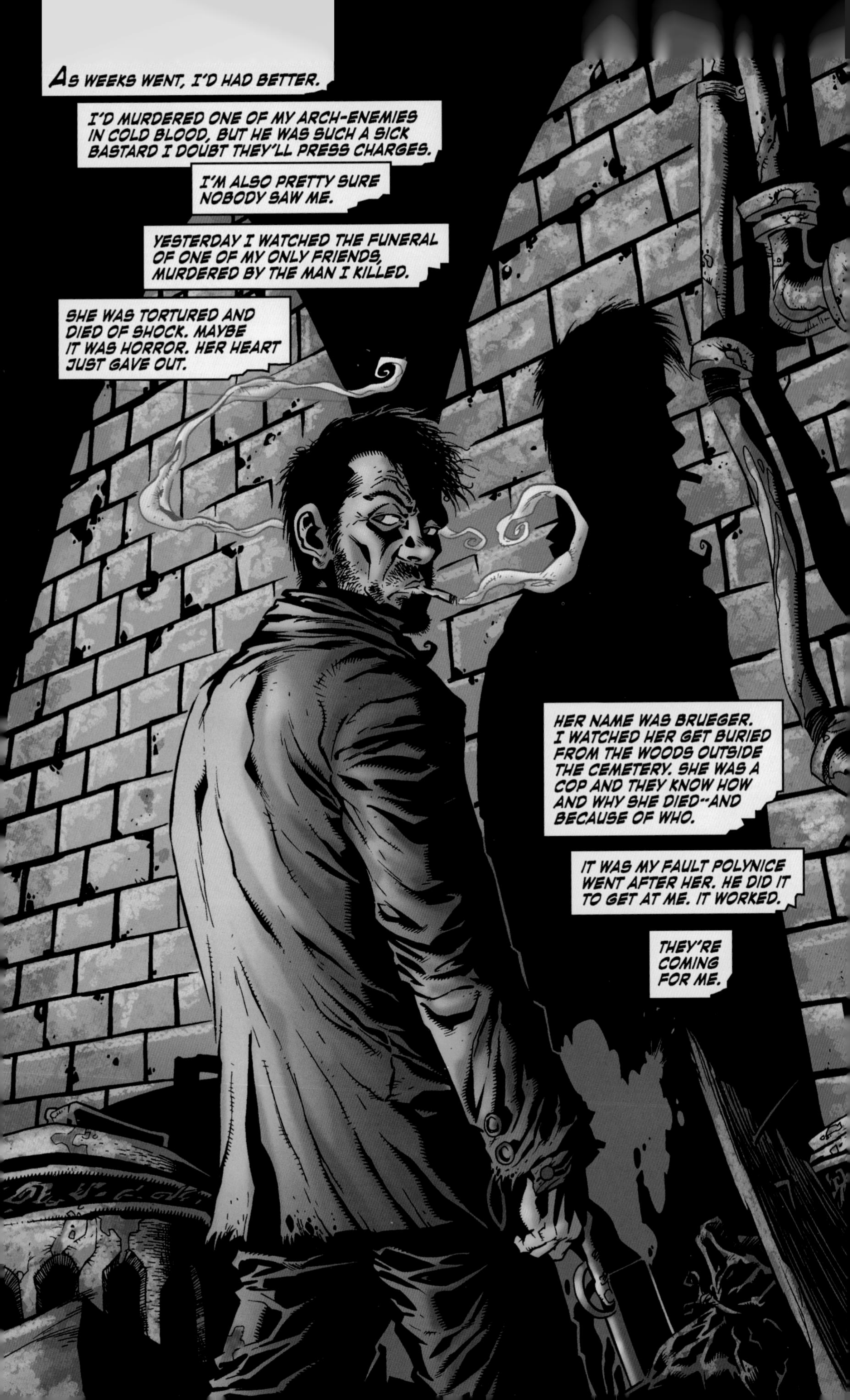
AS WEEKS WENT, I'D HAD BETTER.
I'D MURDERED ONE OF MY ARCH-ENEMIES IN COLD BLOOD, BUT HE WAS SUCH A SICK BASTARD I DOUBT THEY'LL PRESS CHARGES.
I'M ALSO PRETTY SURE NOBODY SAW ME.
YESTERDAY I WATCHED THE FUNERAL OF ONE OF MY ONLY FRIENDS, MURDERED BY THE MAN I KILLED.
SHE WAS TORTURED AND DIED OF SHOCK. MAYBE IT WAS HORROR. HER HEART JUST GAVE OUT.
HER NAME WAS BRUEGER. I WATCHED HER GET BURIED FROM THE WOODS OUTSIDE THE CEMETERY. SHE WAS A COP AND THEY KNOW HOW AND WHY SHE DIED--AND BECAUSE OF WHO.
IT WAS MY FAULT POLYNICE WENT AFTER HER. HE DID IT TO GET AT ME. IT WORKED.
THEY'RE COMING FOR ME.

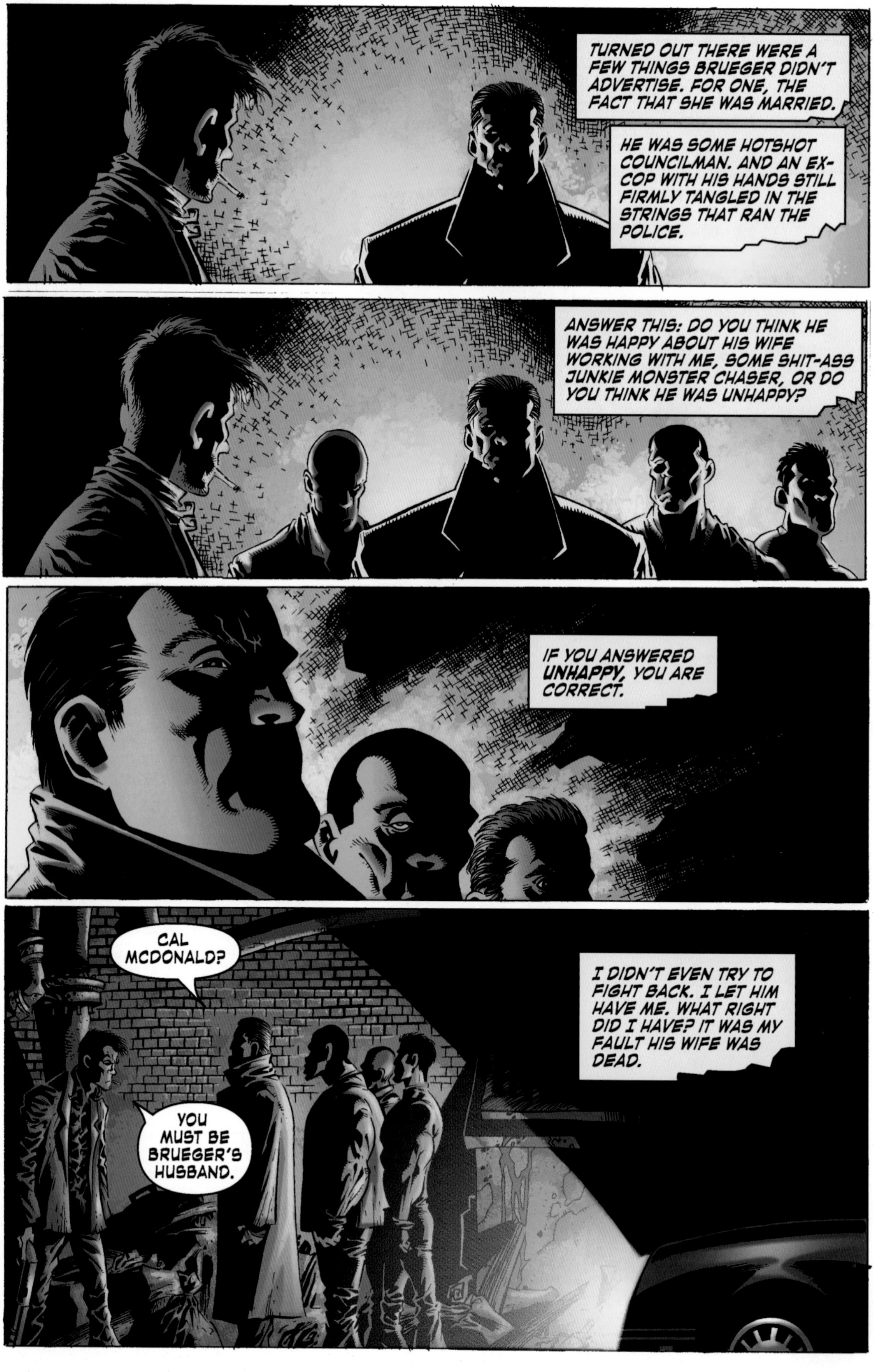
TURNED OUT THERE WERE A FEW THINGS BRUEGER DIDN'T ADVERTISE. FOR ONE, THE FACT THAT SHE WAS MARRIED.
HE WAS SOME HOTSHOT COUNCILMAN. AND AN EX-COP WITH HIS HANDS STILL FIRMLY TANGLED IN THE STRINGS THAT RAN THE POLICE.
ANSWER THIS: DO YOU THINK HE WAS HAPPY ABOUT HIS WIFE WORKING WITH ME, SOME SHIT-ASS JUNKIE MONSTER CHASER, OR DO YOU THINK HE WAS UNHAPPY?
IF YOU ANSWERED UNHAPPY, YOU ARE CORRECT.
CAL MCDONALD?
I DIDN'T EVEN TRY TO FIGHT BACK. I LET HIM HAVE ME. WHAT RIGHT DID I HAVE? IT WAS MY FAULT HIS WIFE WAS DEAD.
YOU MUST BE BRUEGER'S HUSBAND.

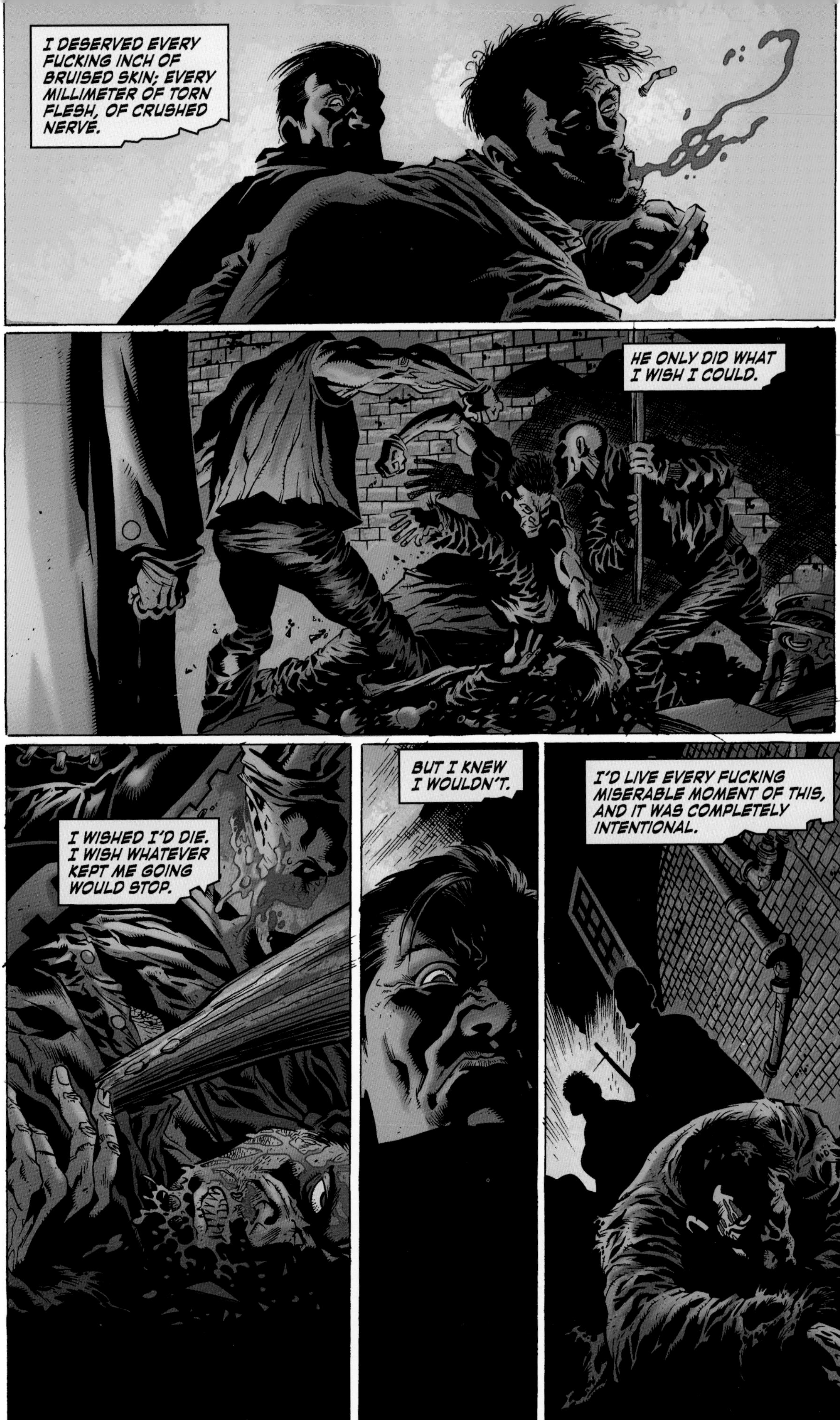
I DESERVED EVERY FUCKING INCH OF BRUISED SKIN; EVERY MILLIMETER OF TORN FLESH, OF CRUSHED NERVE.
HE ONLY DID WHAT I WISH I COULD.
I WISHED I'D DIE. I WISH WHATEVER KEPT ME GOING WOULD STOP.
BUT I KNEW I WOULDN'T.
I'D LIVE EVERY FUCKING MISERABLE MOMENT OF THIS, AND IT WAS COMPLETELY INTENTIONAL.

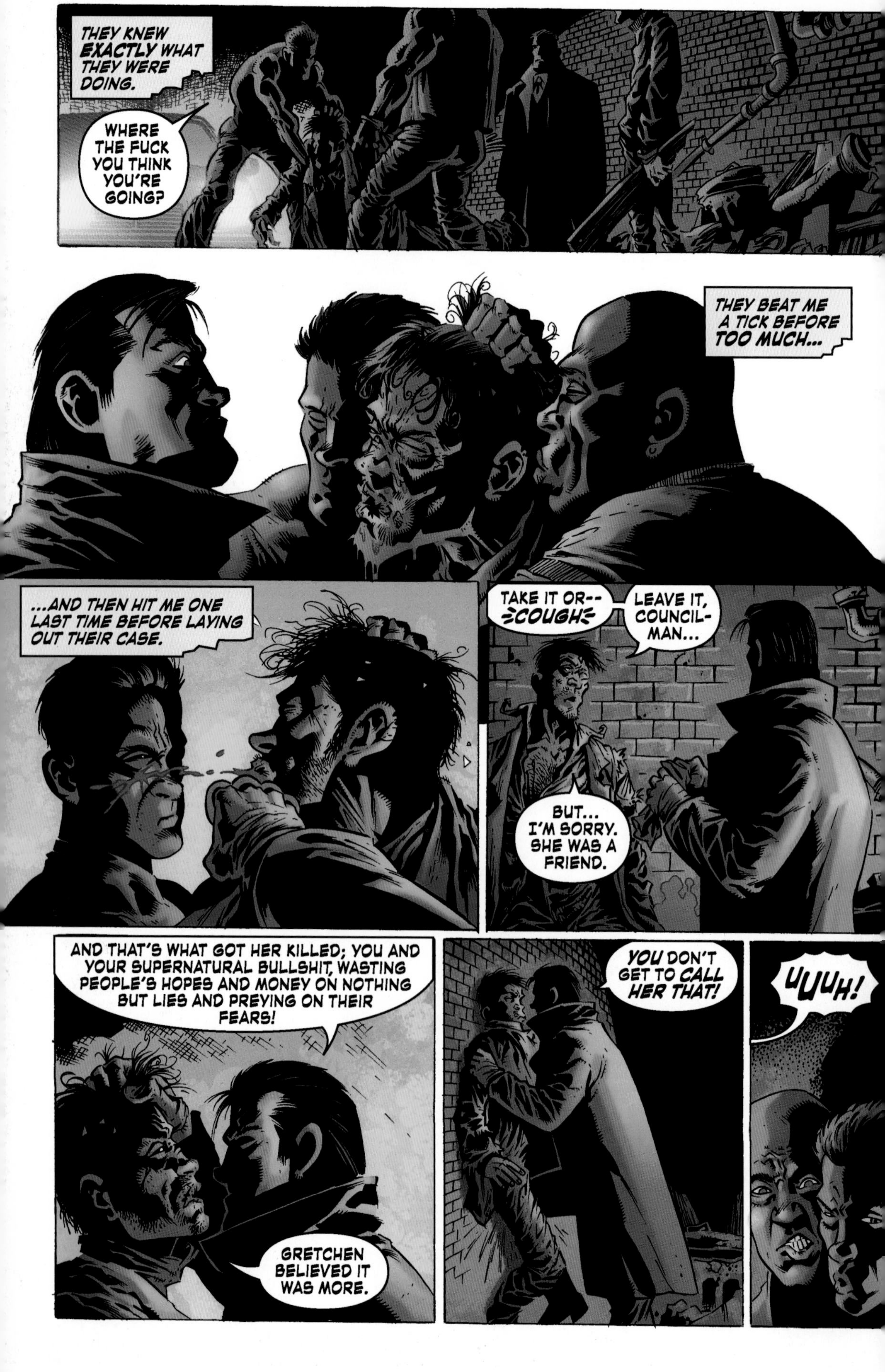
THEY KNEW EXACTLY WHAT THEY WERE DOING.
WHERE THE FUCK YOU THINK YOU'RE GOING?
THEY BEAT ME A TICK BEFORE TOO MUCH...
...AND THEN HIT ME ONE LAST TIME BEFORE LAYING OUT THEIR CASE.
TAKE IT OR-- COUGH
LEAVE IT, COUNCILMAN...
BUT... I'M SORRY. SHE WAS A FRIEND.
AND THAT'S WHAT GOT HER KILLED; YOU AND YOUR SUPERNATURAL BULLSHIT, WASTING PEOPLE'S HOPES AND MONEY ON NOTHING BUT LIES AND PREYING ON THEIR FEARS!
GRETCHEN BELIEVED IT WAS MORE.
YOU DON'T GET TO CALL HER THAT!
UUUH!

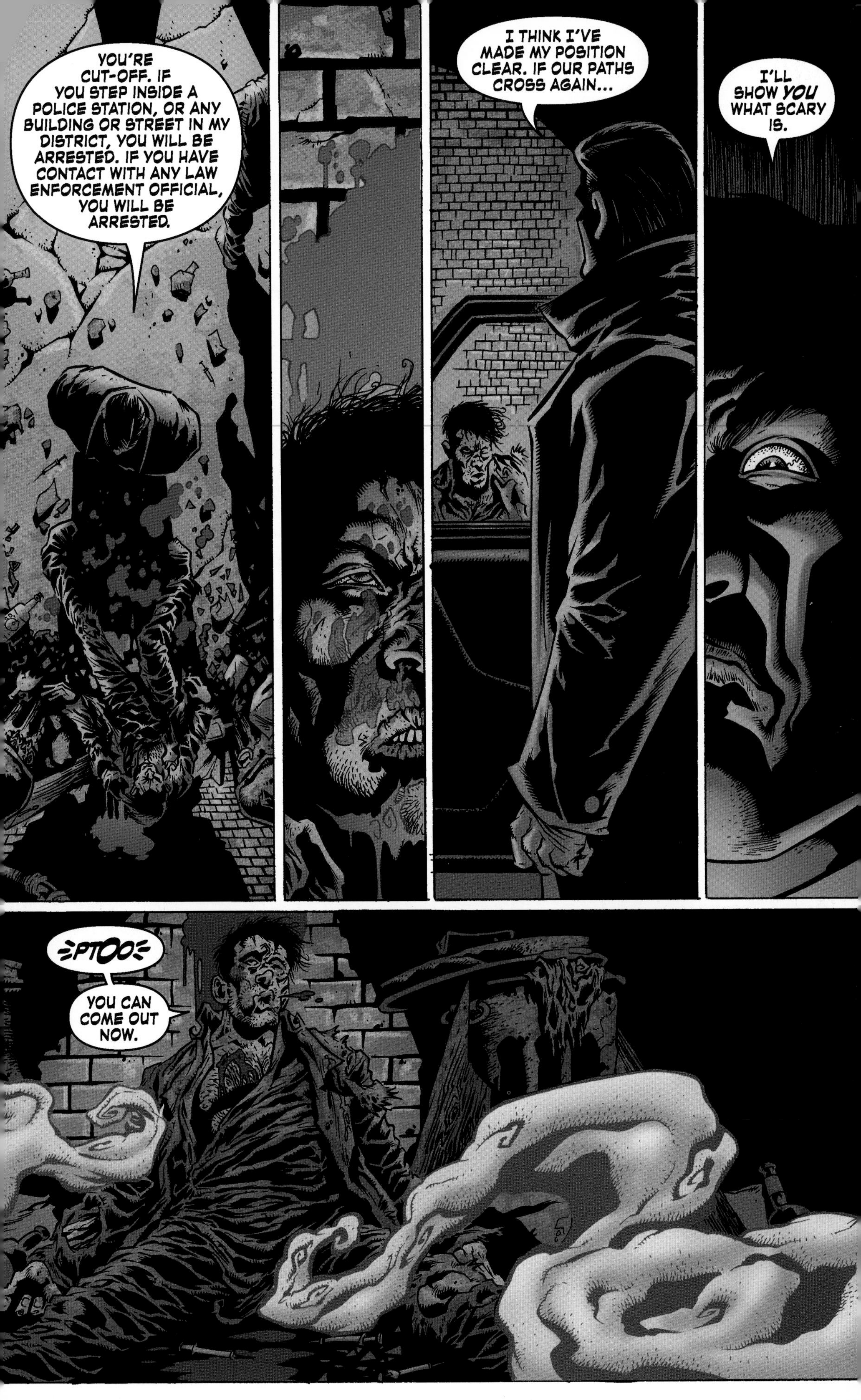
YOU'RE CUT-OFF. IF YOU STEP INSIDE A POLICE STATION, OR ANY BUILDING OR STREET IN MY DISTRICT, YOU WILL BE ARRESTED. IF YOU HAVE CONTACT WITH ANY LAW ENFORCEMENT OFFICIAL, YOU WILL BE ARRESTED.
I THINK I'VE MADE MY POSITION CLEAR. IF OUR PATHS CROSS AGAIN...
I'LL SHOW *YOU* WHAT SCARY IS.
PTOO
YOU CAN COME OUT NOW.

WE COULD NOT HELP YOU. YOU KNOW WE CAN'T ENGAGE HUMANS, ESPECIALLY LAW ENFORCEMENT OFFICERS.
I KNOW, JE'EM. WOULDN'T WANT YOU TO GET YOUR DEAD, NO-LIFE HANDS DIRTY.
I'M GLAD YOU SEE MY POINT, CAL MCDONALD.
I CAME AS SOON AS I COULD. WHAT'S HAPPENED?
TURNS OUT BRUEGER HAD A HUSBAND. LET'S JUST *CHOKE* SAY HE'S NOT MY BIGGEST FAN.
IF I COULD HAVE BEEN HERE I WOULD HAVE.
I KNOW YOU WOULD HAVE, BUDDY. I KNOW.
CAN WE GET ME TO A HOSPITAL? I THINK MY SPLEEN JUST FELL OUT.
SHOULD I CALL SABRINA IN SAN FRANCISCO? PERHAPS SHE WOULD WANT TO KNOW.
SHE DOESN'T GIVE A SHIT. SHE LEFT, REMEMBER?
TAKE ME TO A VETERINARIAN. I DON'T CARE, JUST GET SOMEBODY TO SEW MY ASS UP AND GIVE ME SOME FUCKING PILLS.
I WILL TAKE YOU MYSELF.
HEH, HEH. YEAH, YEAH.

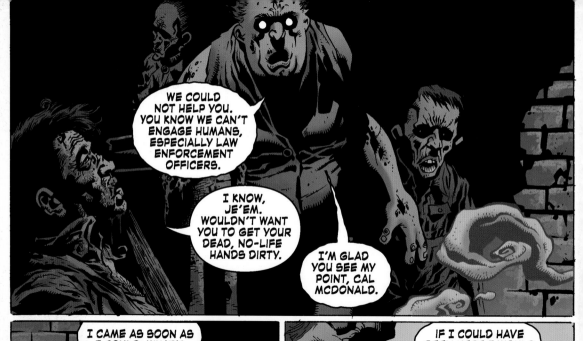

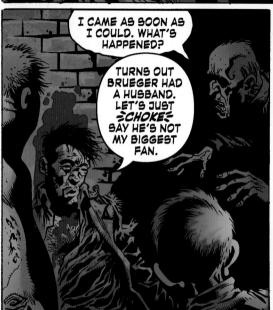

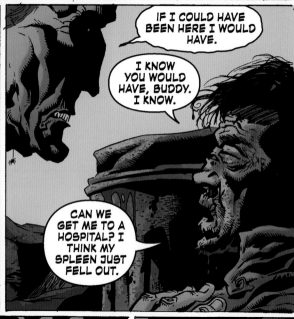

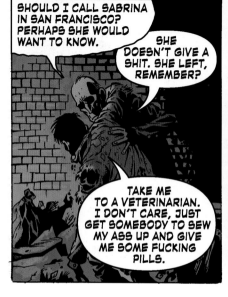

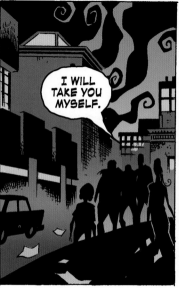

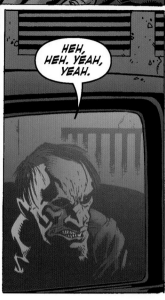

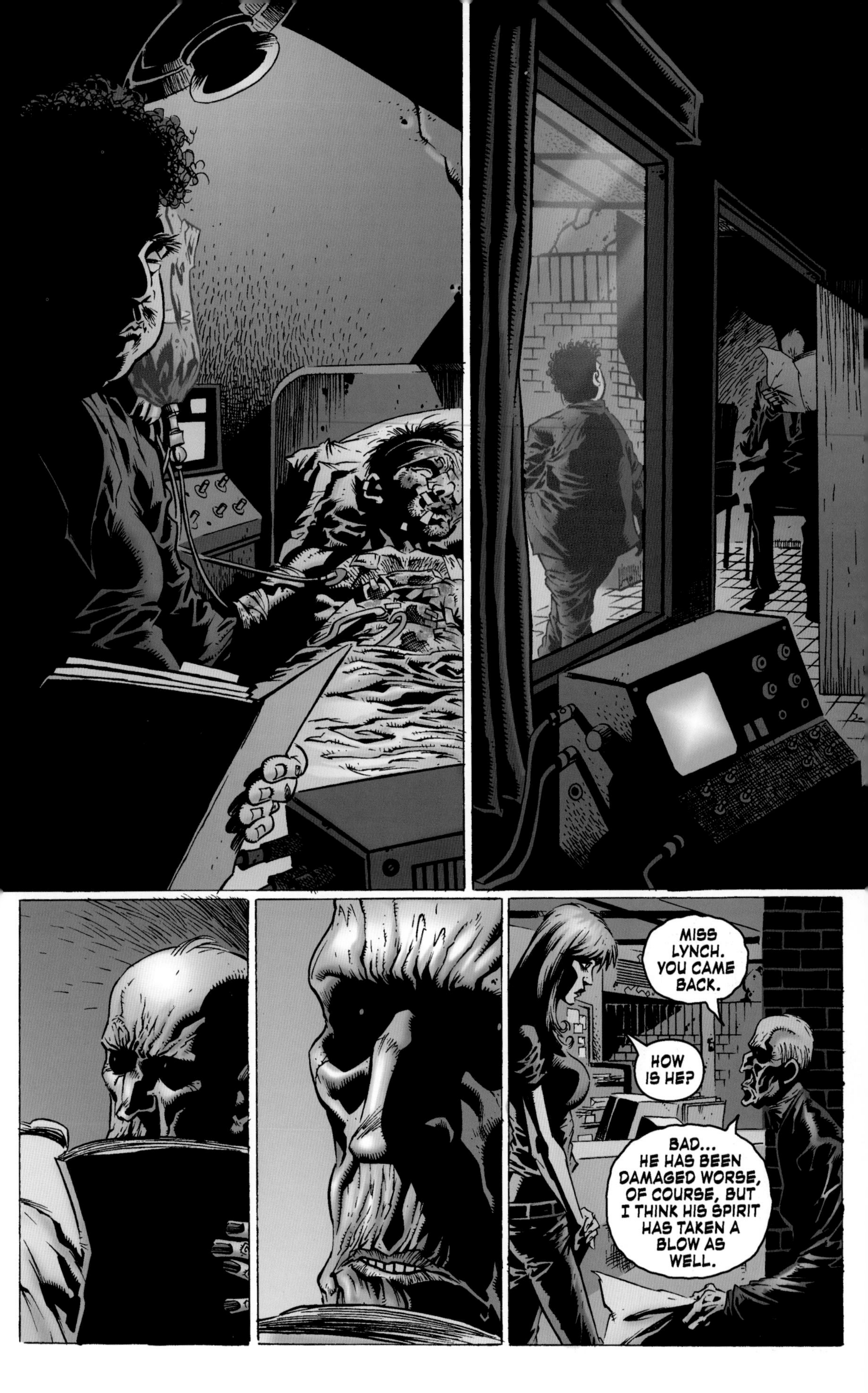
MISS LYNCH. YOU CAME BACK.
HOW IS HE?
BAD... HE HAS BEEN DAMAGED WORSE, OF COURSE, BUT I THINK HIS SPIRIT HAS TAKEN A BLOW AS WELL.

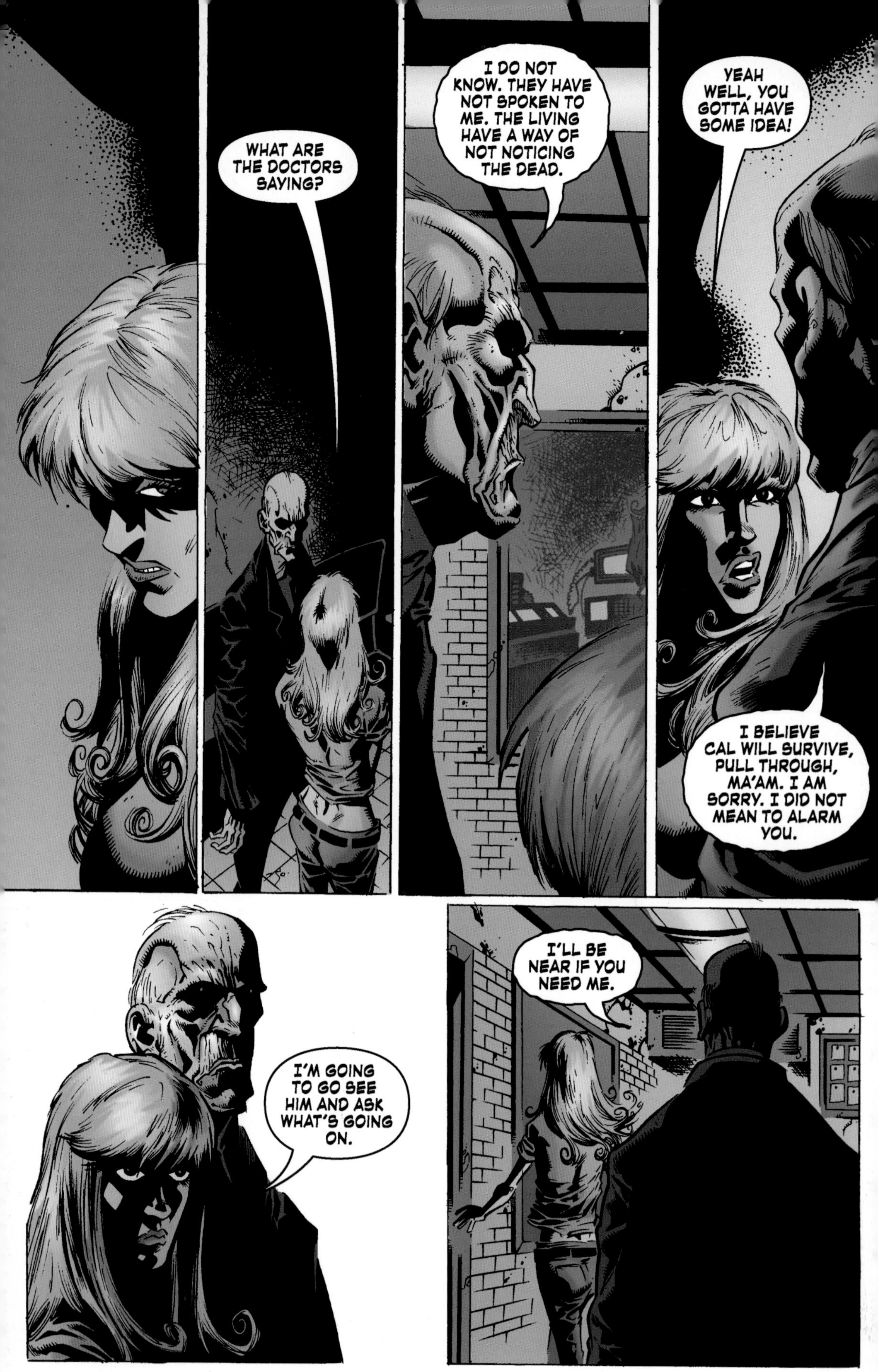
WHAT ARE THE DOCTORS SAYING?
I DO NOT KNOW. THEY HAVE NOT SPOKEN TO ME. THE LIVING HAVE A WAY OF NOT NOTICING THE DEAD.
YEAH WELL, YOU GOTTA HAVE SOME IDEA!
I BELIEVE CAL WILL SURVIVE, PULL THROUGH, MA'AM. I AM SORRY. I DID NOT MEAN TO ALARM YOU.
I'M GOING TO GO SEE HIM AND ASK WHAT'S GOING ON.
I'LL BE NEAR IF YOU NEED ME.

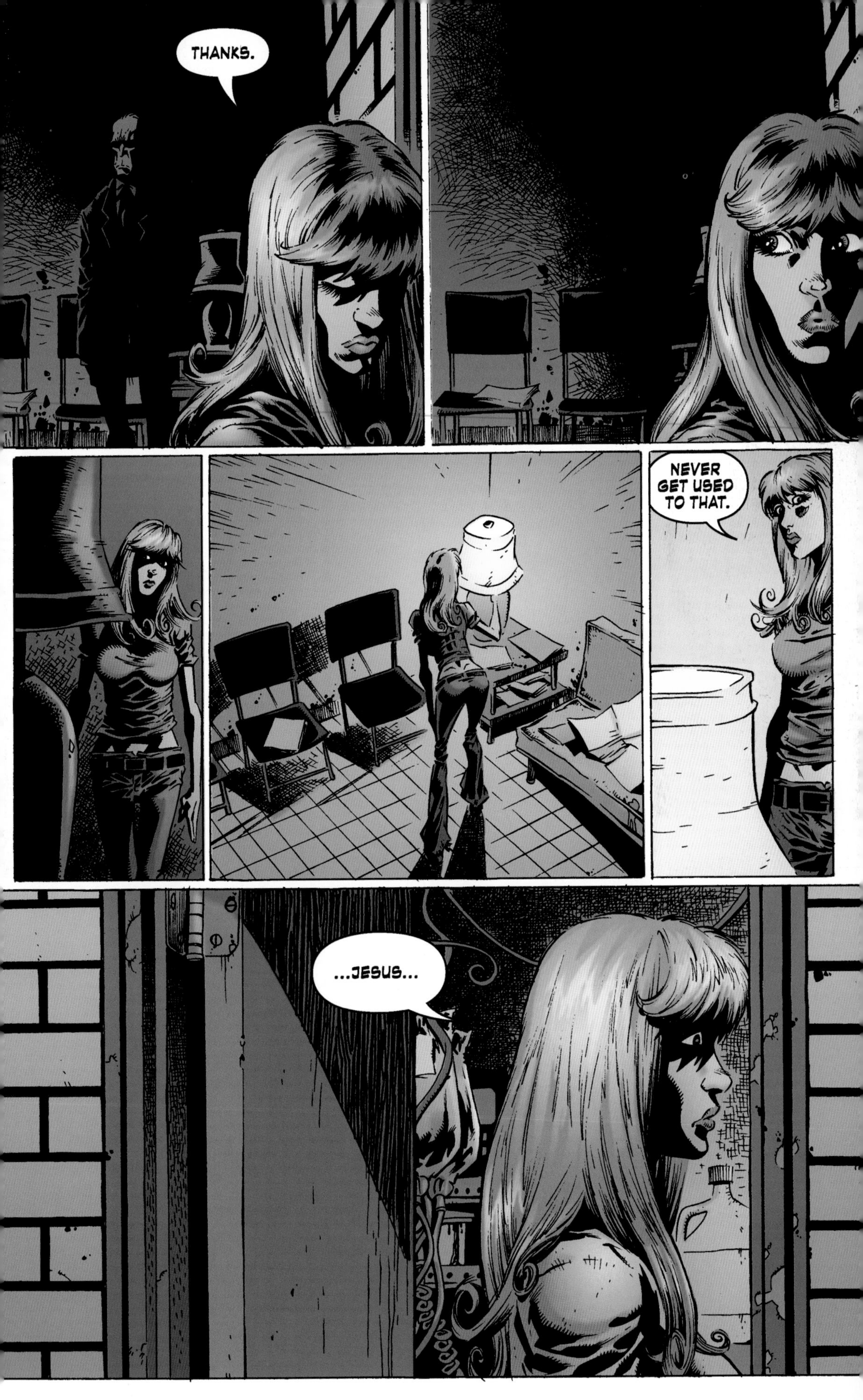
THANKS.
NEVER GET USED TO THAT.
...JESUS...

JE'EM. WHAT BRINGS YOU HERE? I HAVE ALL THE SECURITY FORCES I REQUIRE TO KEEP CAL SAFE.

THERE IS ANOTHER REASON I HAVE COME.

THIS IS PA'TTON. HE WAS WALKED ALL THE WAY FROM WASHINGTON DC WITH A MESSAGE FROM THE RESIDENT GHOULS.

PA'TTON, THIS IS MO'LOCK, THE CLOSE ASSOCIATE OF CAL MCDONALD.

IT IS A PLEASURE TO MEET YOU, BROTHER.

THERE ARE FEW WHO ARE UNAWARE OF MO'LOCK.

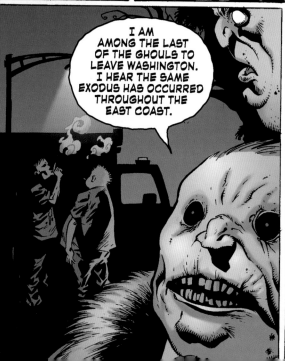

I AM AMONG THE LAST OF THE GHOULS TO LEAVE WASHINGTON. I HEAR THE SAME EXODUS HAS OCCURRED THROUGHOUT THE EAST COAST.

EXODUS OF GHOULS? WHERE ARE THEY ALL GOING?

THEY ARE ALL COMING HERE... TO CAL MCDONALD.

I LEFT YOU A MESSAGE. I LEFT IT ON THE PHONE AT THE HOUSE THAT GOT LEVELED WHEN LIEUTENANT BRUEGER WAS KILLED.

LOOK AT YOU.

I KNOW, IN THAT BIG, STUBBORN HEAD OF YOURS, YOU THINK I LEFT YOU BECAUSE I WAS AFRAID OF GETTING KILLED. BUT IT'S THE OTHER WAY AROUND. I DIDN'T WANT TO SIT AND WAIT FOR YOU TO GET KILLED OR KILL YOURSELF OR SOME BIZARRE DRUG-INDUCED COMBINATION OF THE TWO.

I WAS GETTING TO THE POINT WHERE I COULDN'T HANDLE THE THOUGHT OF YOU DYING, AND YOU GAVE ME TOO MANY REASONS TO WORRY. YOU THINK YOU'RE BIG AND BRAVE, BUT THE TRUTH IS YOU'RE A SUICIDAL MANIAC.

I WOULD HAVE STAYED IN L.A. WITH YOU, IF I THOUGHT YOU WANTED TO LIVE. I'M NOT SURE YOU DO.

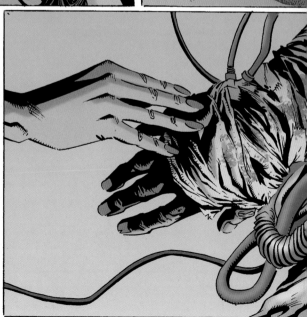

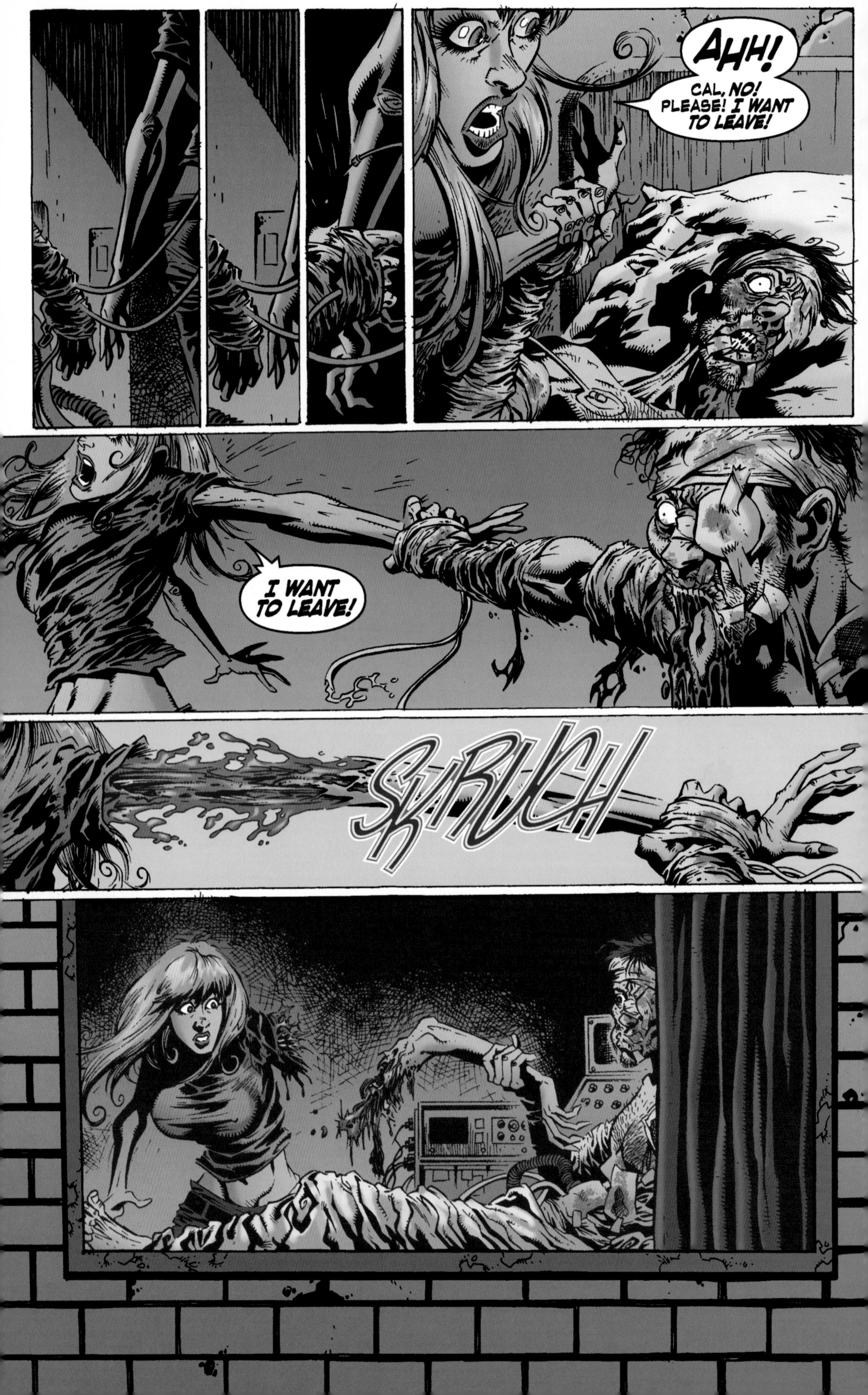
AHH!
CAL, NO! PLEASE! I WANT TO LEAVE!
I WANT TO LEAVE!
SKRUCH

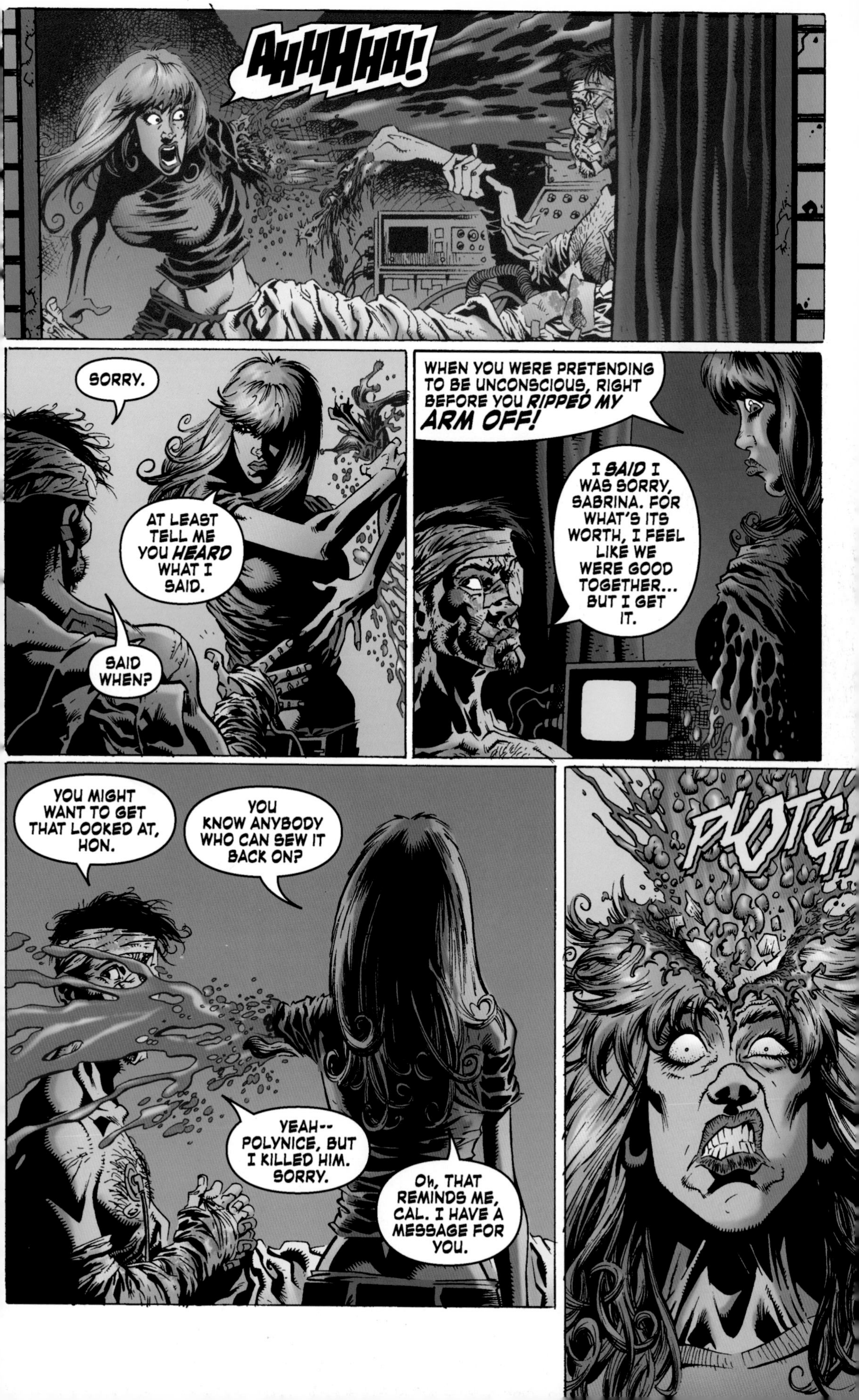
AHHHHH!
SORRY.
AT LEAST TELL ME YOU **HEARD** WHAT I SAID.
SAID WHEN?
WHEN YOU WERE PRETENDING TO BE UNCONSCIOUS, RIGHT BEFORE YOU ***RIPPED MY ARM OFF!***
I **SAID** I WAS SORRY, SABRINA. FOR WHAT'S ITS WORTH, I FEEL LIKE WE WERE GOOD TOGETHER... BUT I GET IT.
YOU MIGHT WANT TO GET THAT LOOKED AT, HON.
YOU KNOW ANYBODY WHO CAN SEW IT BACK ON?
YEAH-- POLYNICE, BUT I KILLED HIM. SORRY.
Oh, THAT REMINDS ME, CAL. I HAVE A MESSAGE FOR YOU.
PLOTCH

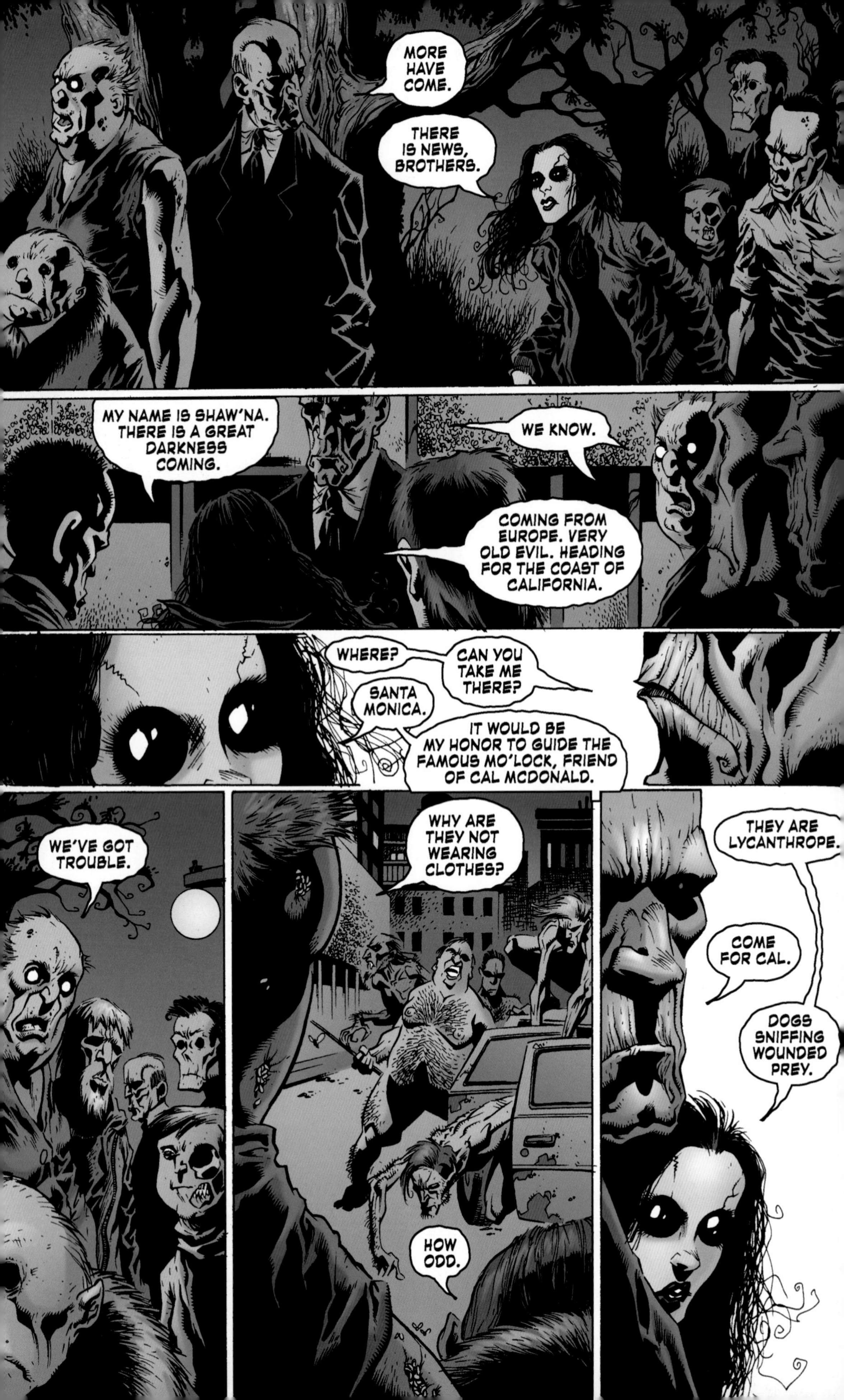
MORE HAVE COME.
THERE IS NEWS, BROTHERS.
MY NAME IS SHAW'NA. THERE IS A GREAT DARKNESS COMING.
WE KNOW.
COMING FROM EUROPE. VERY OLD EVIL. HEADING FOR THE COAST OF CALIFORNIA.
WHERE?
CAN YOU TAKE ME THERE?
SANTA MONICA.
IT WOULD BE MY HONOR TO GUIDE THE FAMOUS MO'LOCK, FRIEND OF CAL MCDONALD.
WE'VE GOT TROUBLE.
WHY ARE THEY NOT WEARING CLOTHES?
HOW ODD.
THEY ARE LYCANTHROPE.
COME FOR CAL.
DOGS SNIFFING WOUNDED PREY.

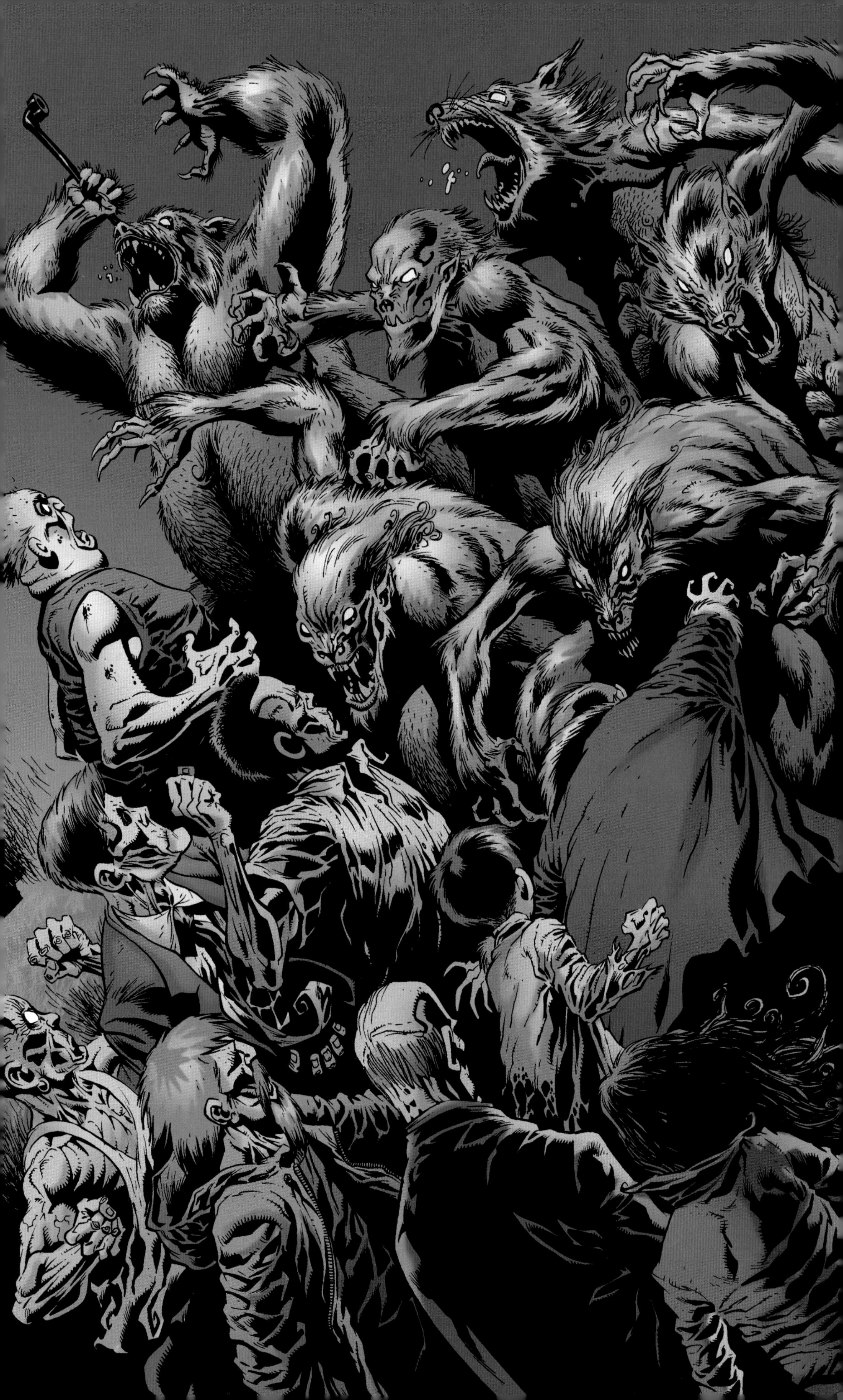

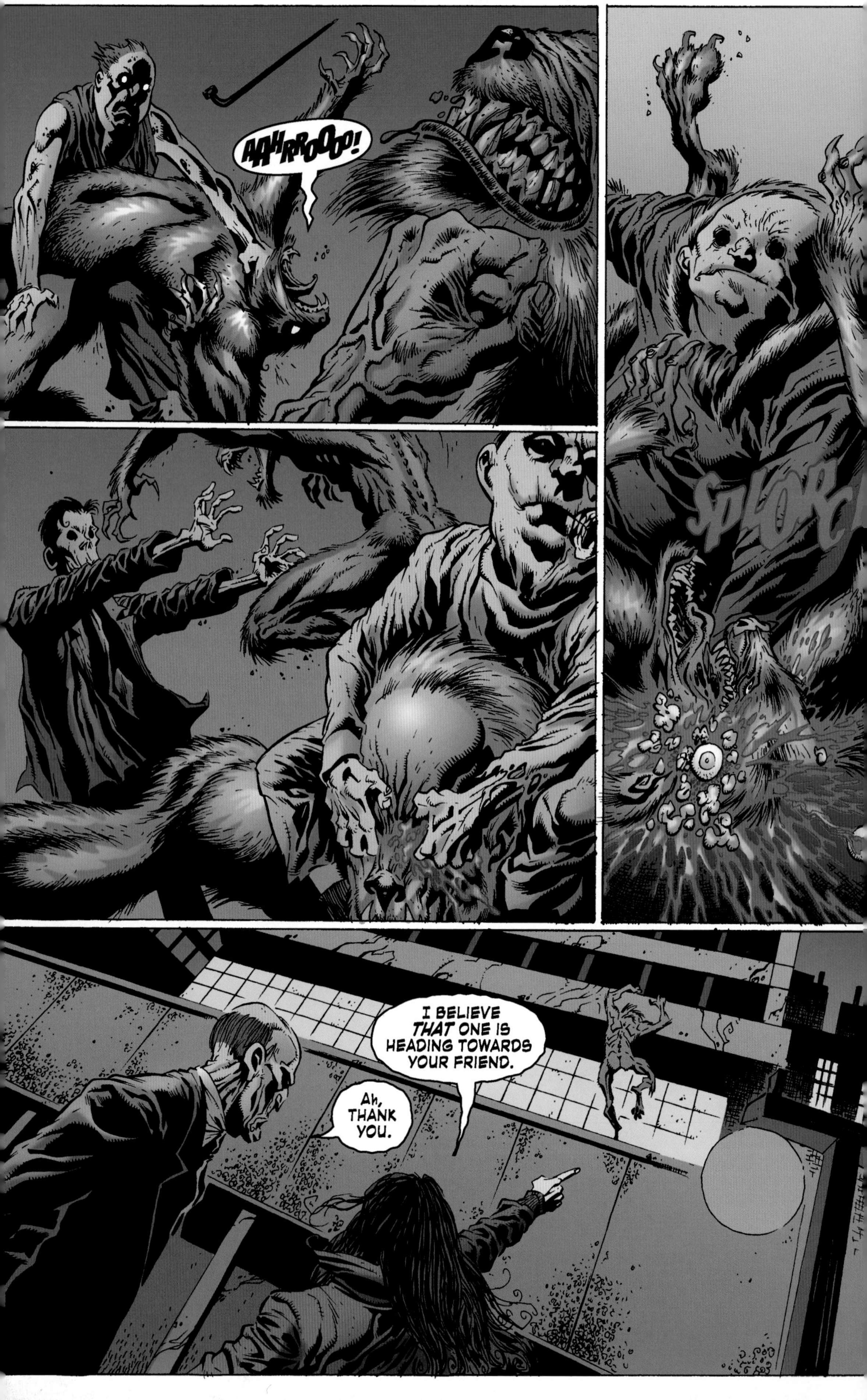
AAHRROOOO!
SPLORC
I BELIEVE THAT ONE IS HEADING TOWARDS YOUR FRIEND.
Ah, THANK YOU.

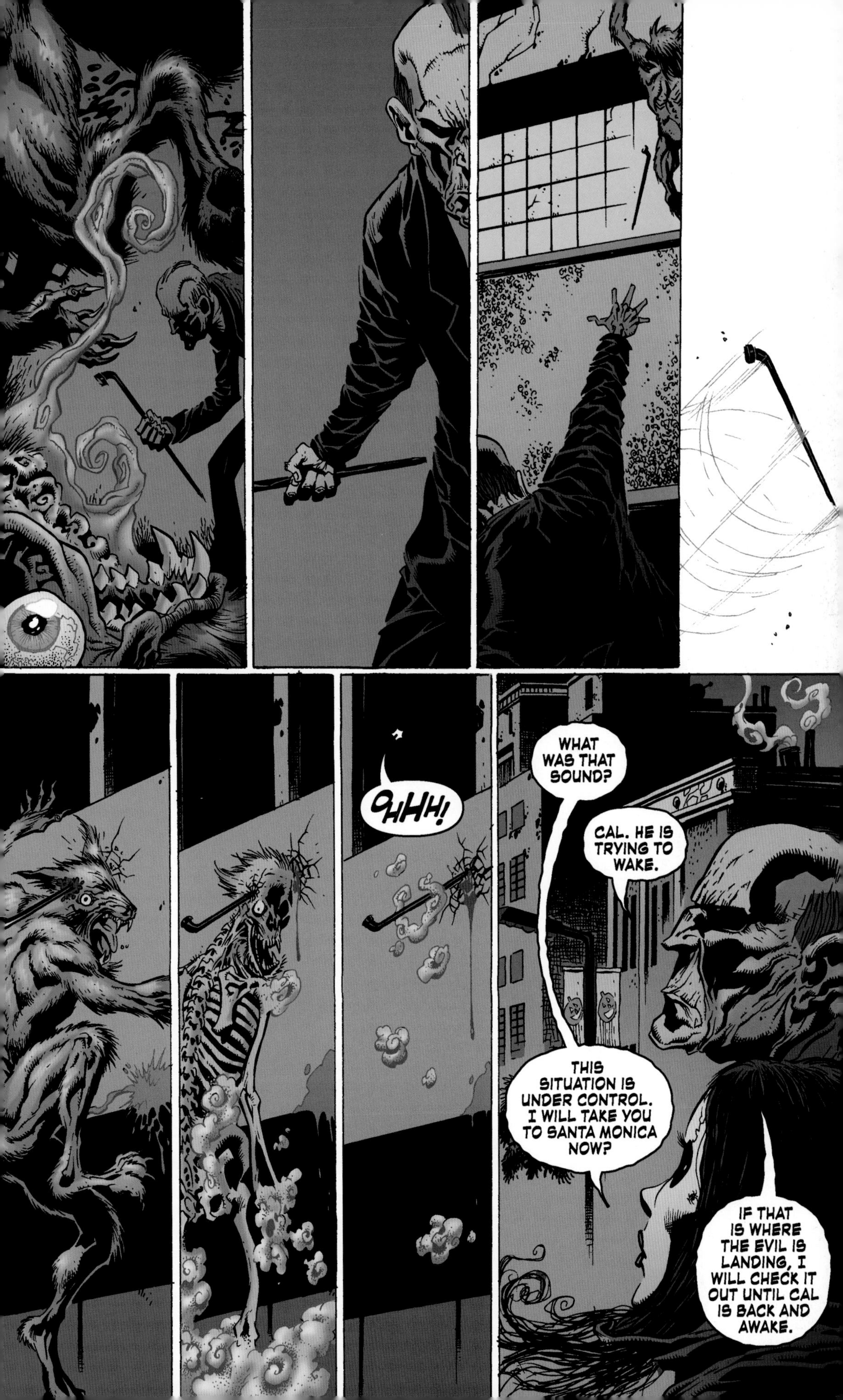
OHHH!
WHAT WAS THAT SOUND?
CAL. HE IS TRYING TO WAKE.
THIS SITUATION IS UNDER CONTROL. I WILL TAKE YOU TO SANTA MONICA NOW?
IF THAT IS WHERE THE EVIL IS LANDING, I WILL CHECK IT OUT UNTIL CAL IS BACK AND AWAKE.

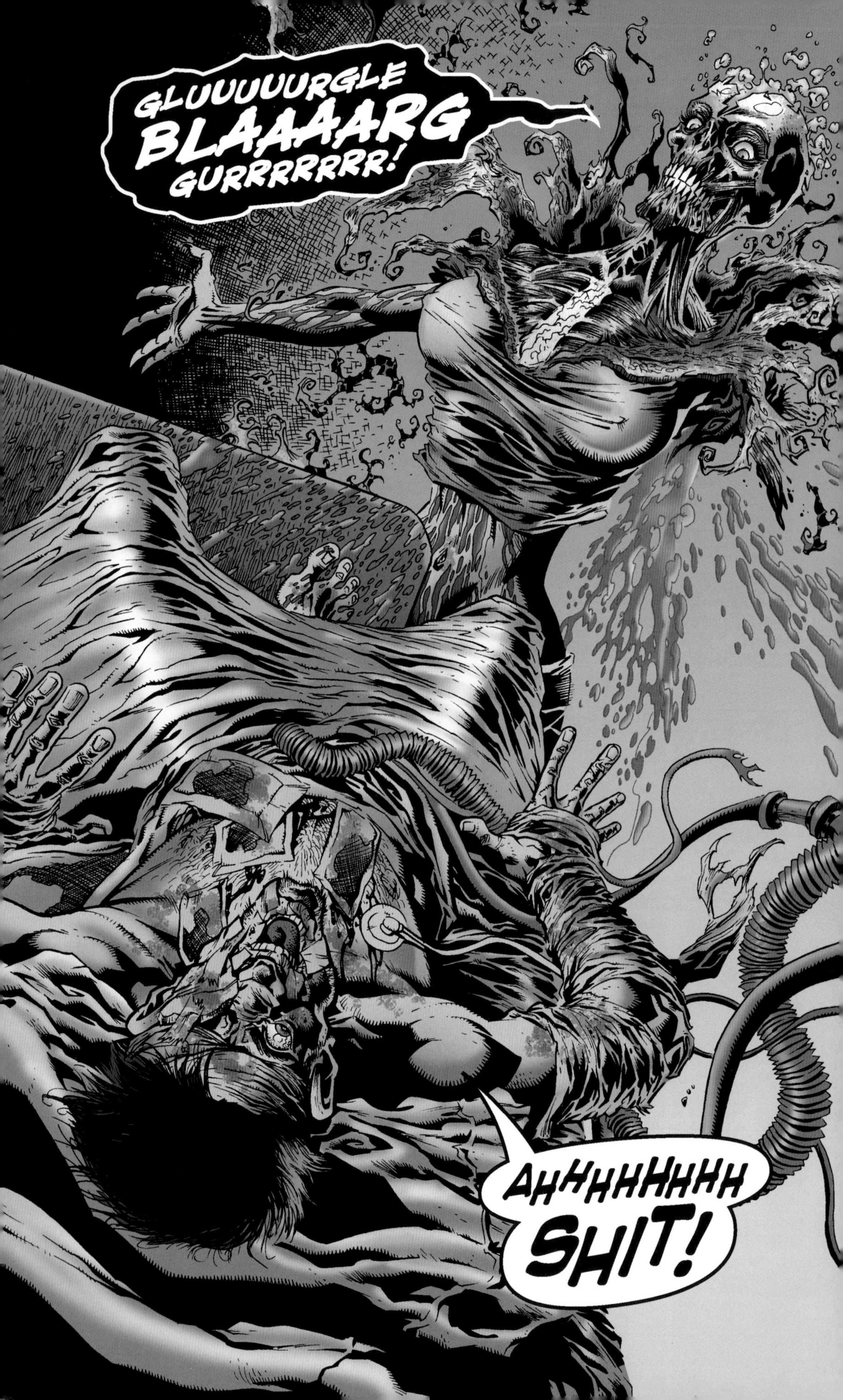
GLUUUUURGLE BLAAAARG GURRRRRRR!
AHHHHHHHH SHIT!

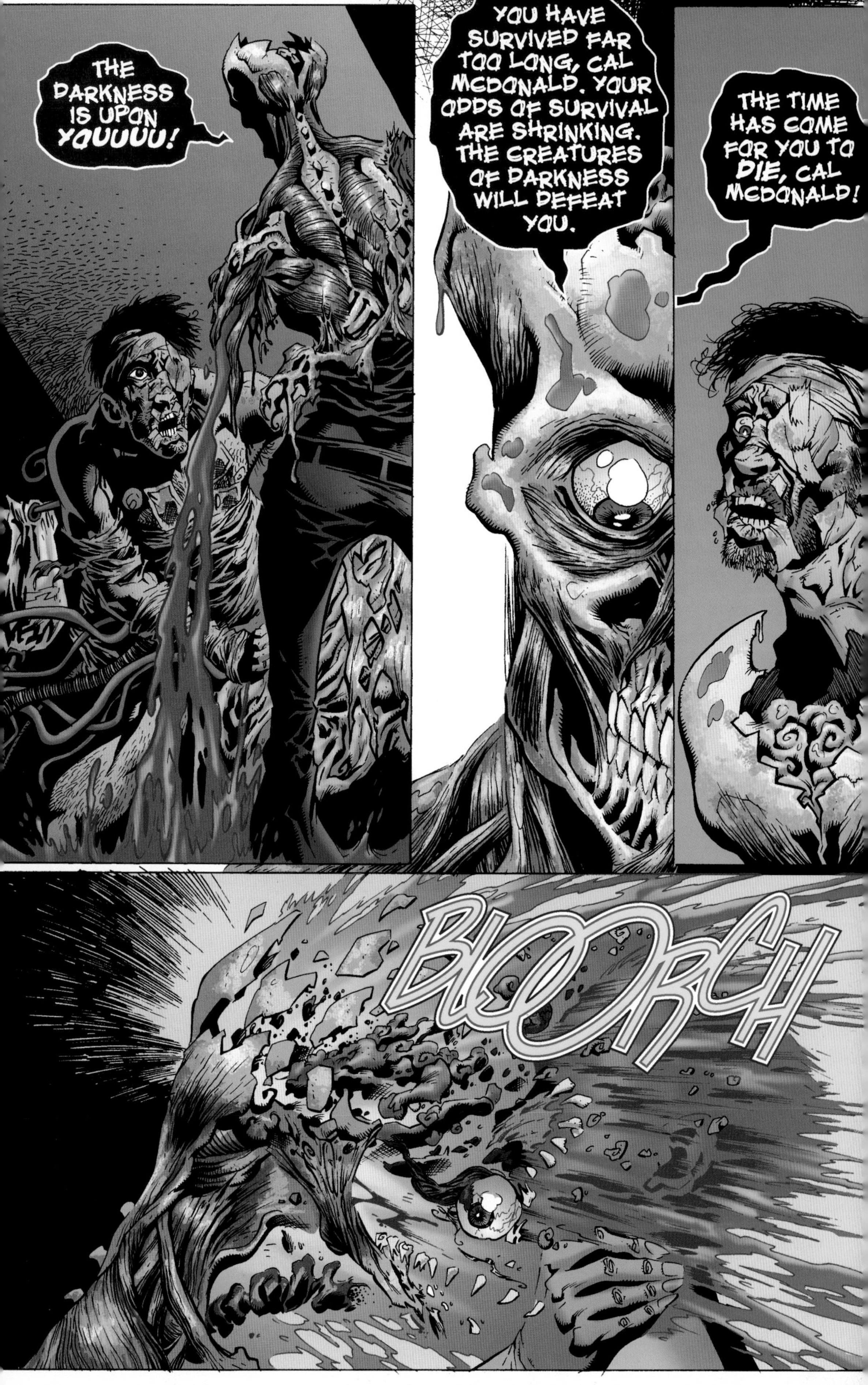
THE DARKNESS IS UPON YOUUUU!
YOU HAVE SURVIVED FAR TOO LONG, CAL McDONALD. YOUR ODDS OF SURVIVAL ARE SHRINKING. THE CREATURES OF DARKNESS WILL DEFEAT YOU.
THE TIME HAS COME FOR YOU TO DIE, CAL McDONALD!
BLOORCH

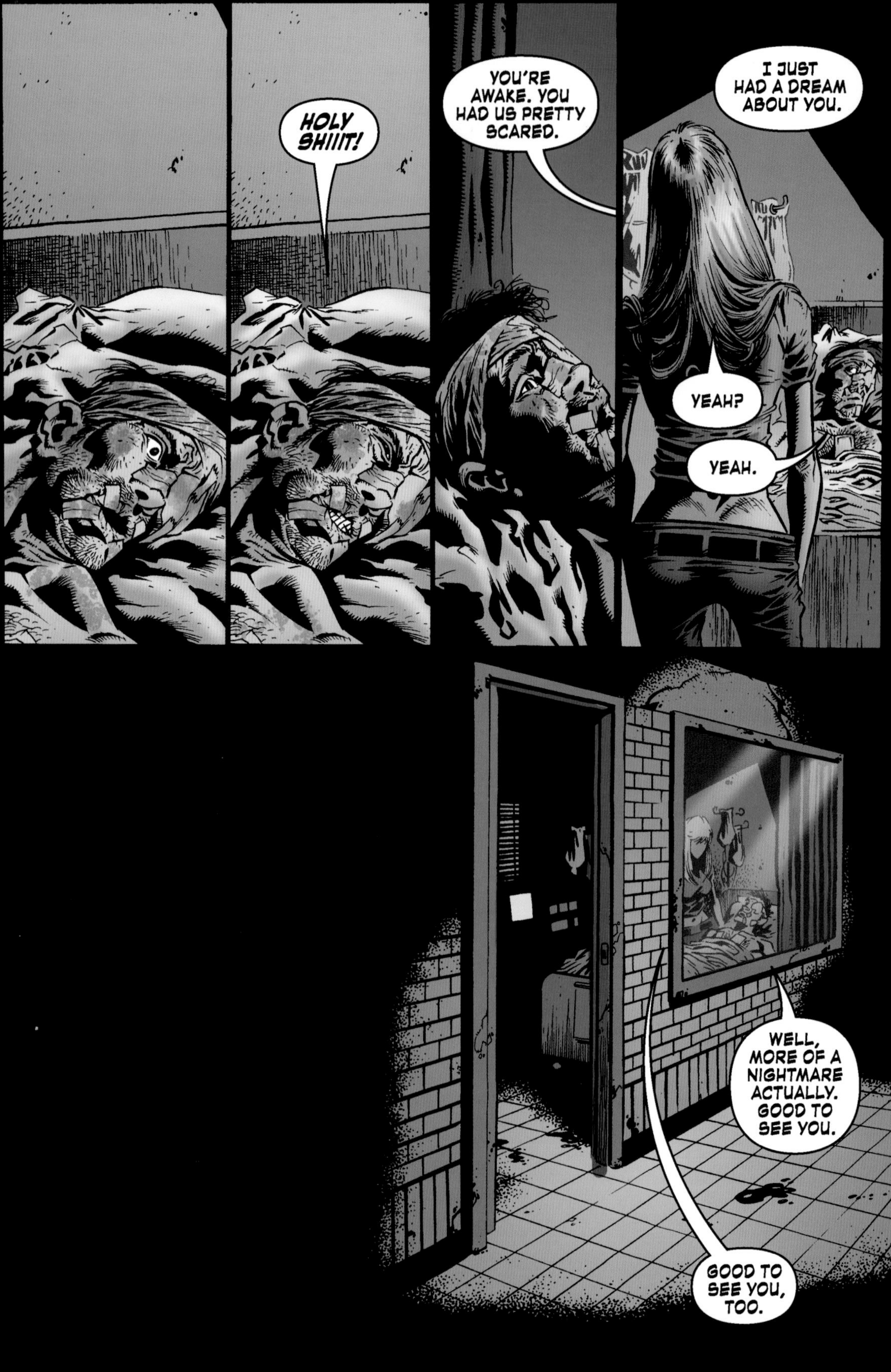
HOLY SHIIIT!
YOU'RE AWAKE. YOU HAD US PRETTY SCARED.
I JUST HAD A DREAM ABOUT YOU.
YEAH?
YEAH.
WELL, MORE OF A NIGHTMARE ACTUALLY. GOOD TO SEE YOU.
GOOD TO SEE YOU, TOO.

WHY ARE WE HERE?

THIS IS WHERE THE PRESENCE IS COMING FROM.

THERE, ON THE OCEAN.

WHAT IS IT?

WHATEVER IT IS, IT'S HUGE.

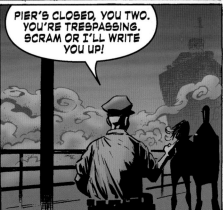

PIER'S CLOSED, YOU TWO. YOU'RE TRESPASSING. SCRAM OR I'LL WRITE YOU UP!

OH... MY...GOD... IT AIN'T GONNA STOP.

I DO NOT BELIEVE SO.

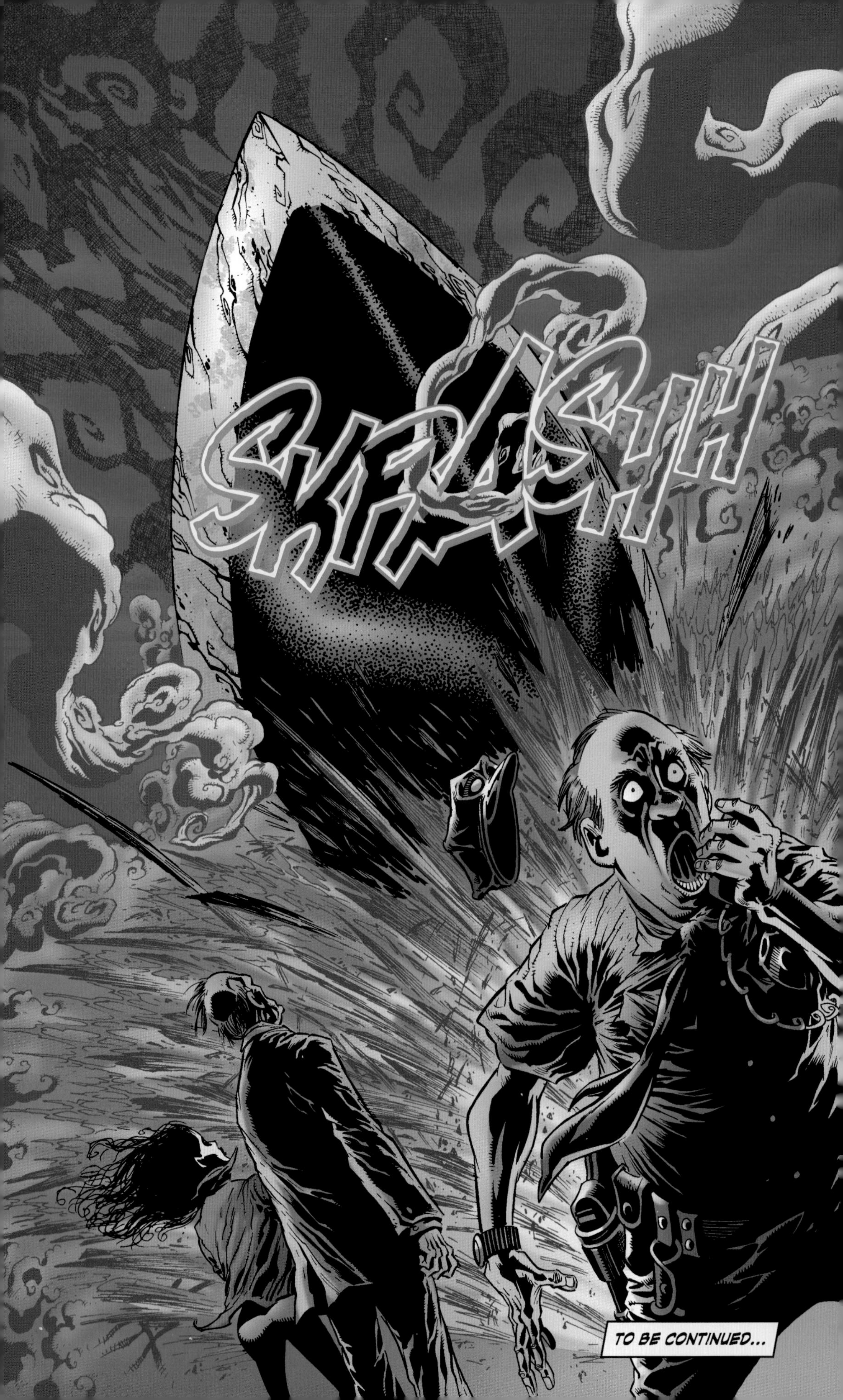
SKRASH
TO BE CONTINUED...

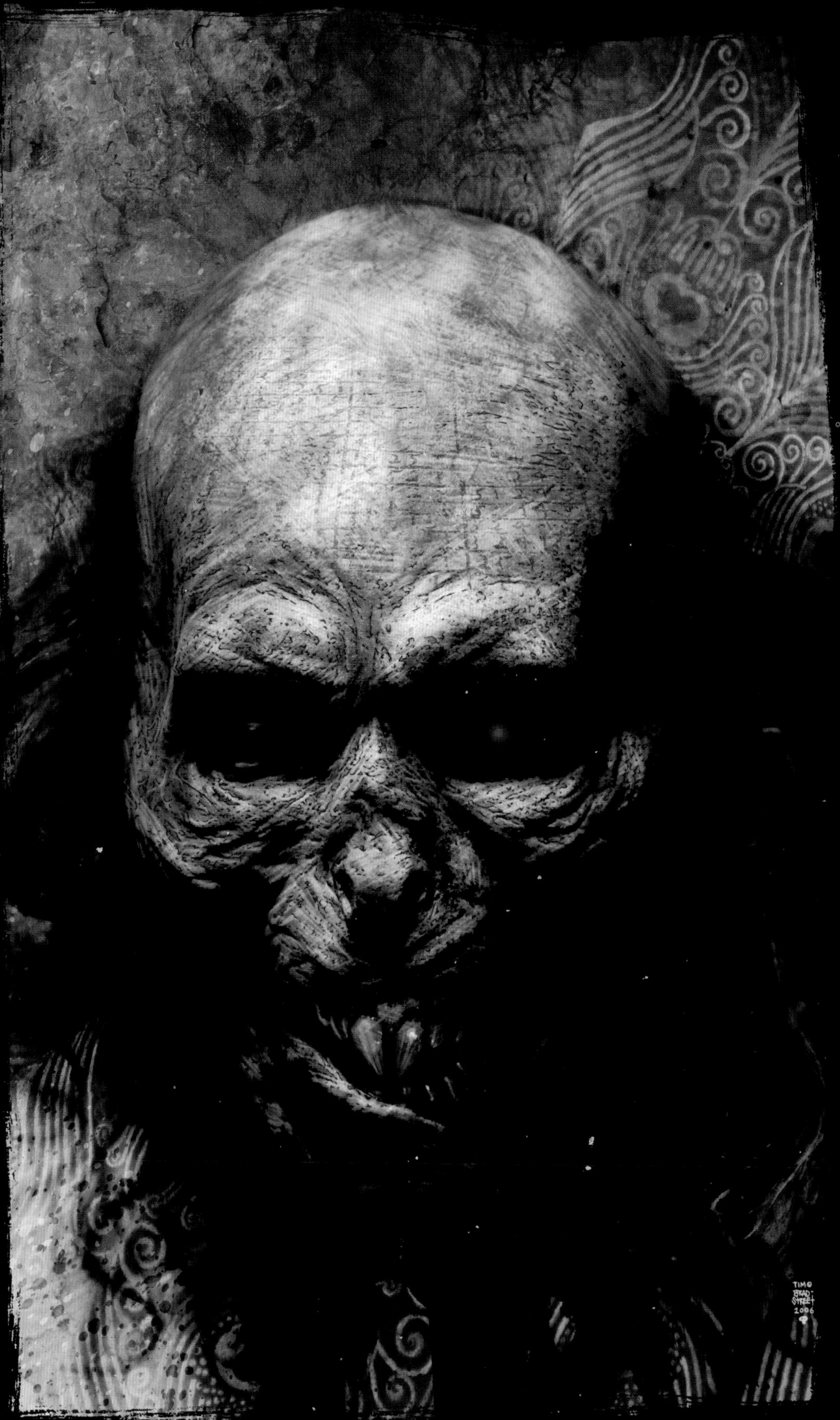
TIMO
BRAD-
STREET
2006

CHAPTER TWO

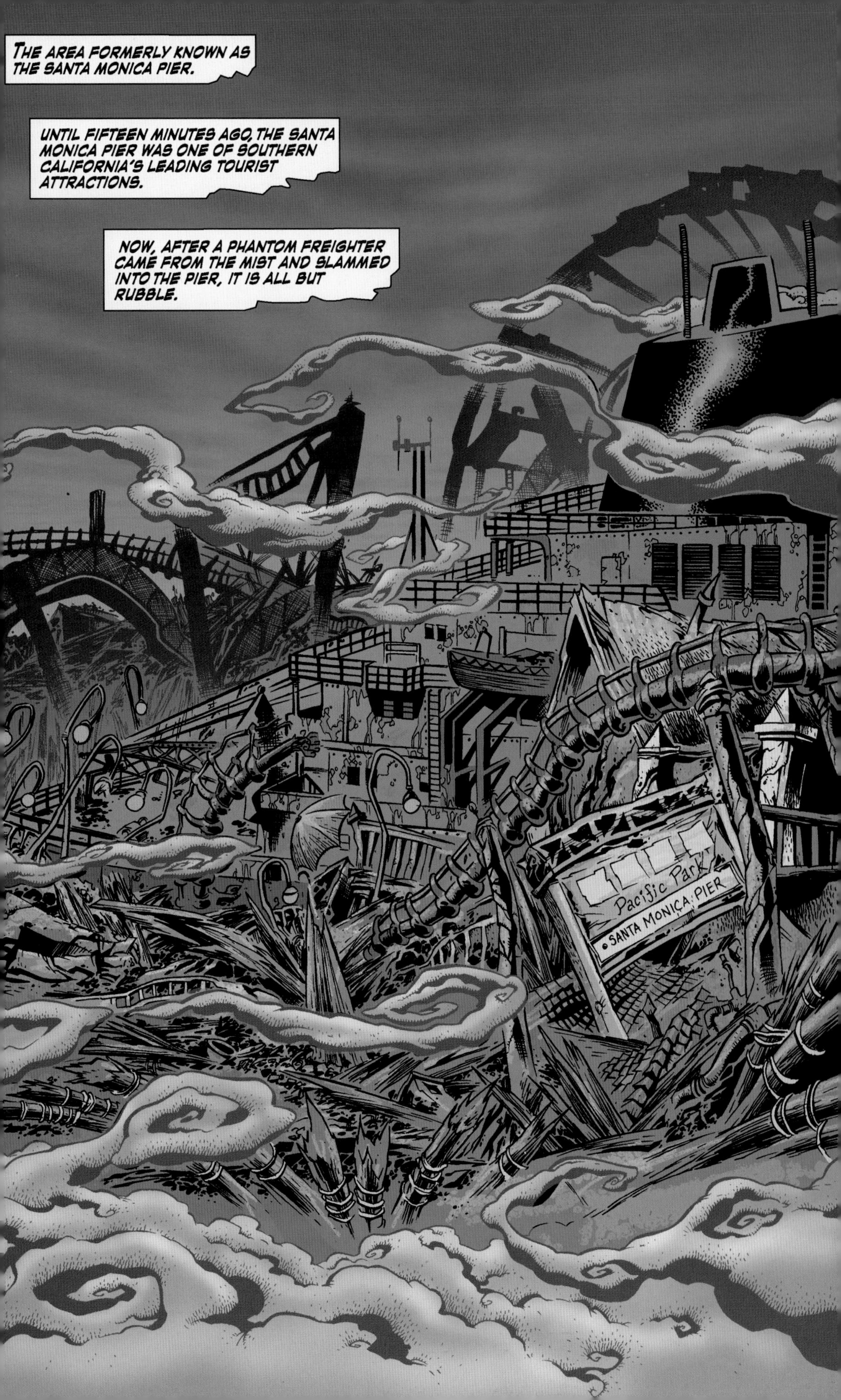
THE AREA FORMERLY KNOWN AS THE SANTA MONICA PIER.
UNTIL FIFTEEN MINUTES AGO, THE SANTA MONICA PIER WAS ONE OF SOUTHERN CALIFORNIA'S LEADING TOURIST ATTRACTIONS.
NOW, AFTER A PHANTOM FREIGHTER CAME FROM THE MIST AND SLAMMED INTO THE PIER, IT IS ALL BUT RUBBLE.
Pacific Park
SANTA MONICA PIER

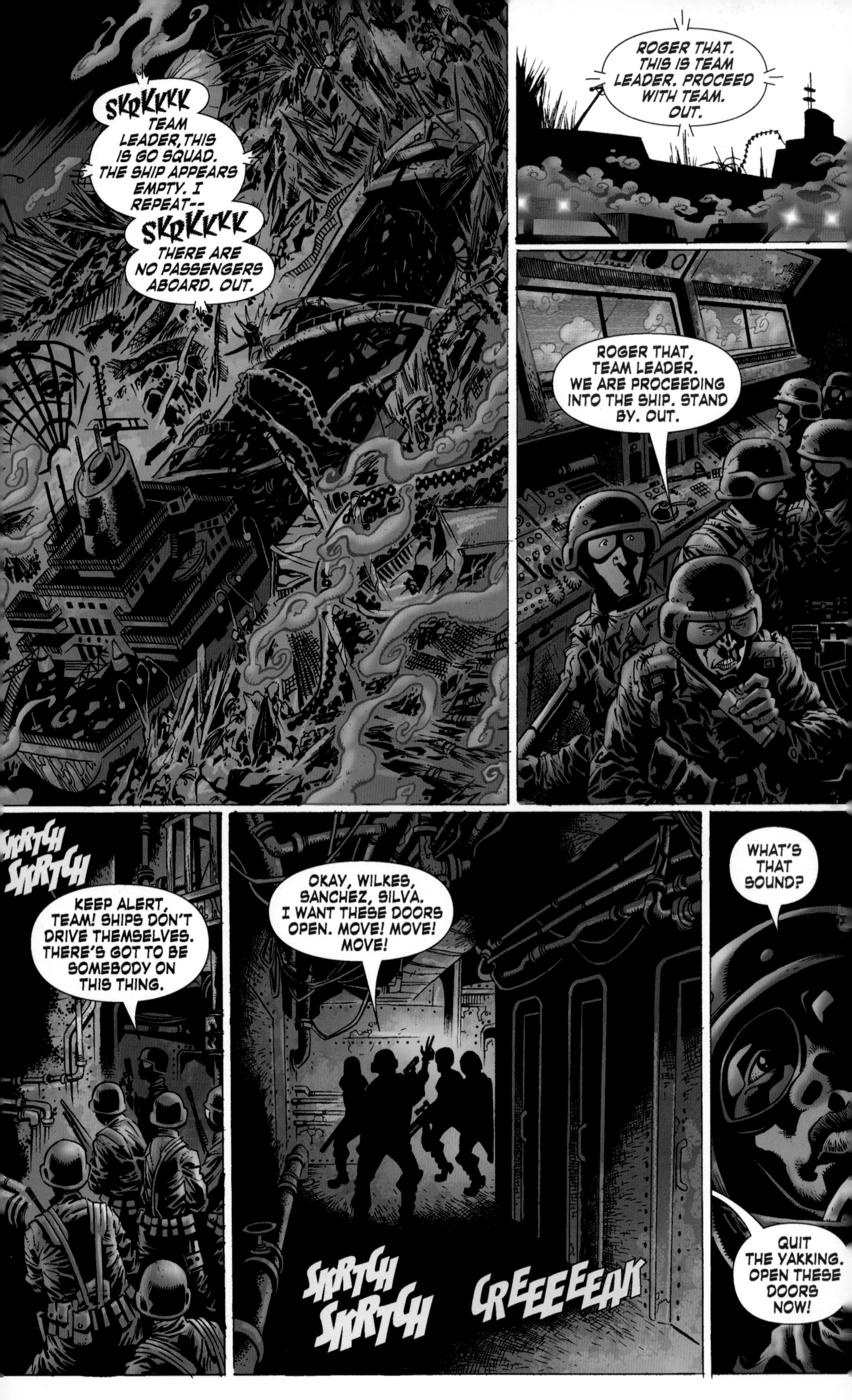

SKRKKKK TEAM LEADER, THIS IS GO SQUAD. THE SHIP APPEARS EMPTY. I REPEAT--
SKRKKKK THERE ARE NO PASSENGERS ABOARD. OUT.
ROGER THAT. THIS IS TEAM LEADER. PROCEED WITH TEAM. OUT.
ROGER THAT, TEAM LEADER. WE ARE PROCEEDING INTO THE SHIP. STAND BY. OUT.
SKRTCH SKRTCH
KEEP ALERT, TEAM! SHIPS DON'T DRIVE THEMSELVES. THERE'S GOT TO BE SOMEBODY ON THIS THING.
OKAY, WILKES, SANCHEZ, SILVA. I WANT THESE DOORS OPEN. MOVE! MOVE! MOVE!
SKRTCH SKRTCH
CREEEEEAK
WHAT'S THAT SOUND?
QUIT THE YAKKING. OPEN THESE DOORS NOW!

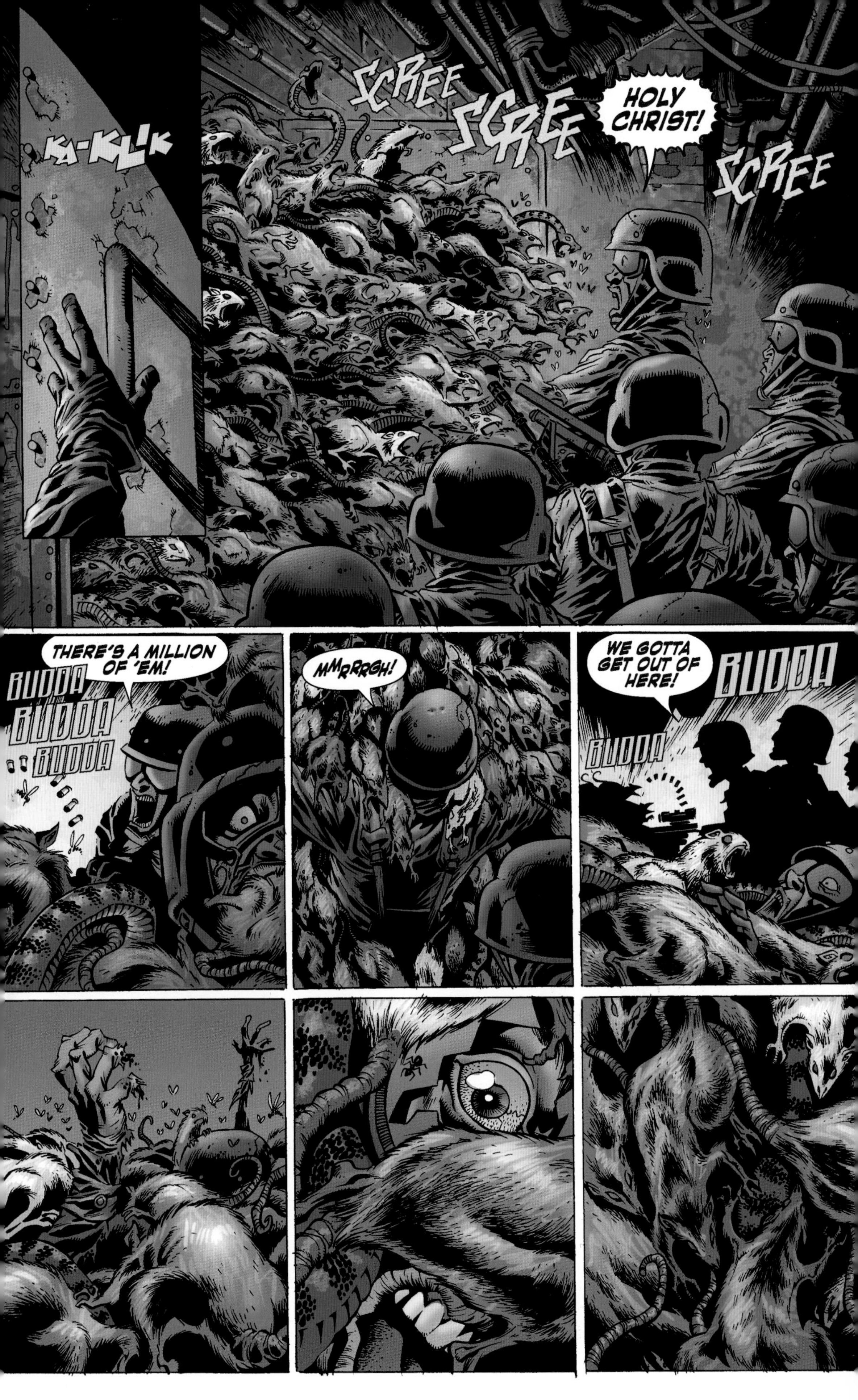
KA-KLIK
SCREE
SCREE
HOLY CHRIST!
SCREE
BUDDA BUDDA BUDDA
THERE'S A MILLION OF 'EM!
MMRRRGH!
WE GOTTA GET OUT OF HERE!
BUDDA
BUDDA

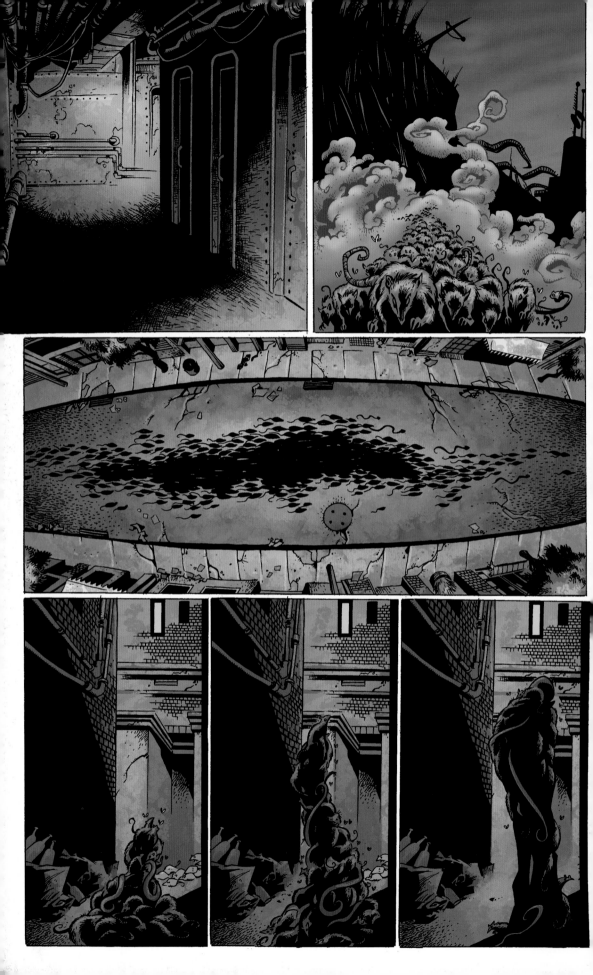

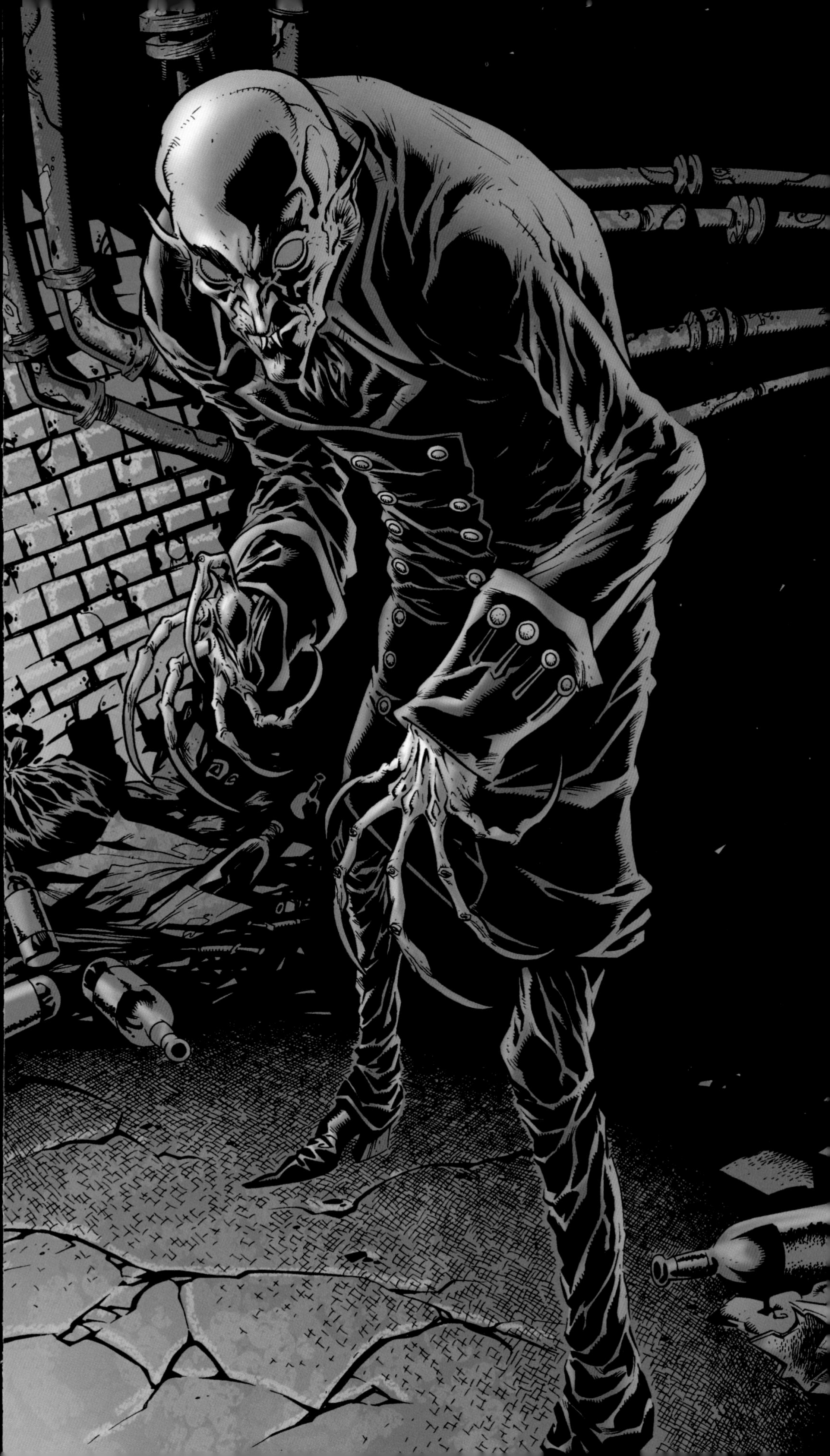

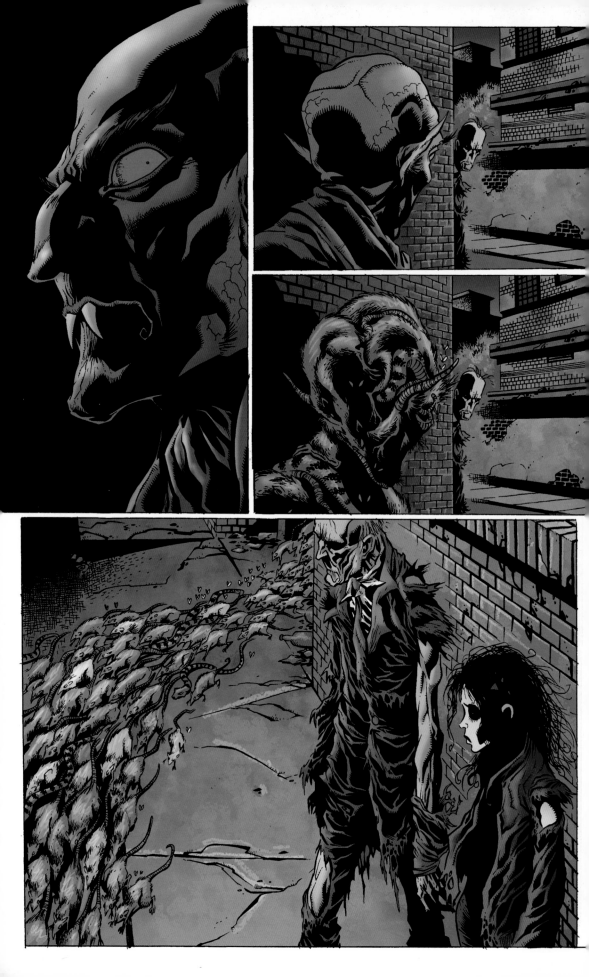

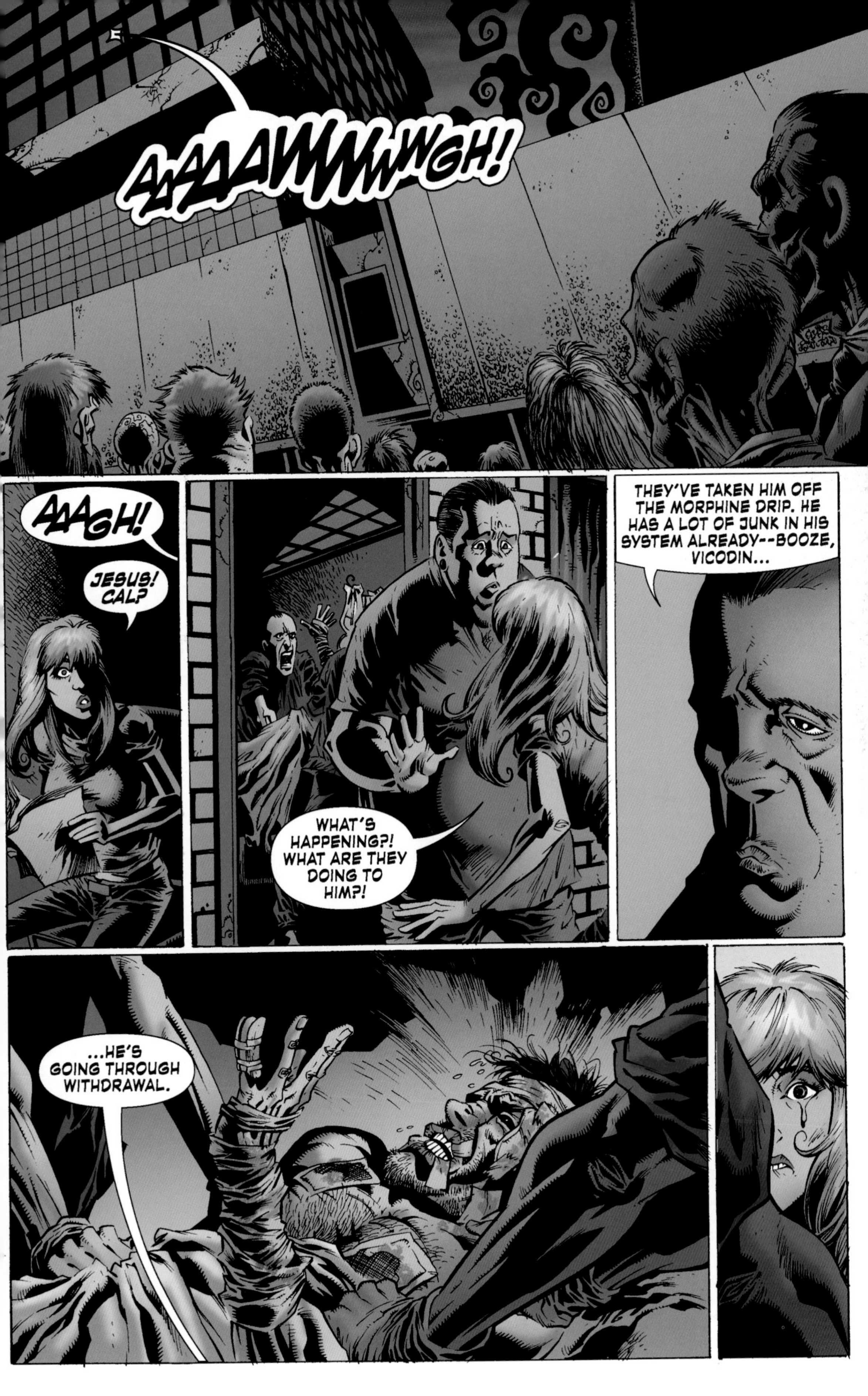
AAAAAWWWWWGH!
AAAGH!
JESUS! CAL?
WHAT'S HAPPENING?! WHAT ARE THEY DOING TO HIM?!
THEY'VE TAKEN HIM OFF THE MORPHINE DRIP. HE HAS A LOT OF JUNK IN HIS SYSTEM ALREADY--BOOZE, VICODIN...
...HE'S GOING THROUGH WITHDRAWAL.

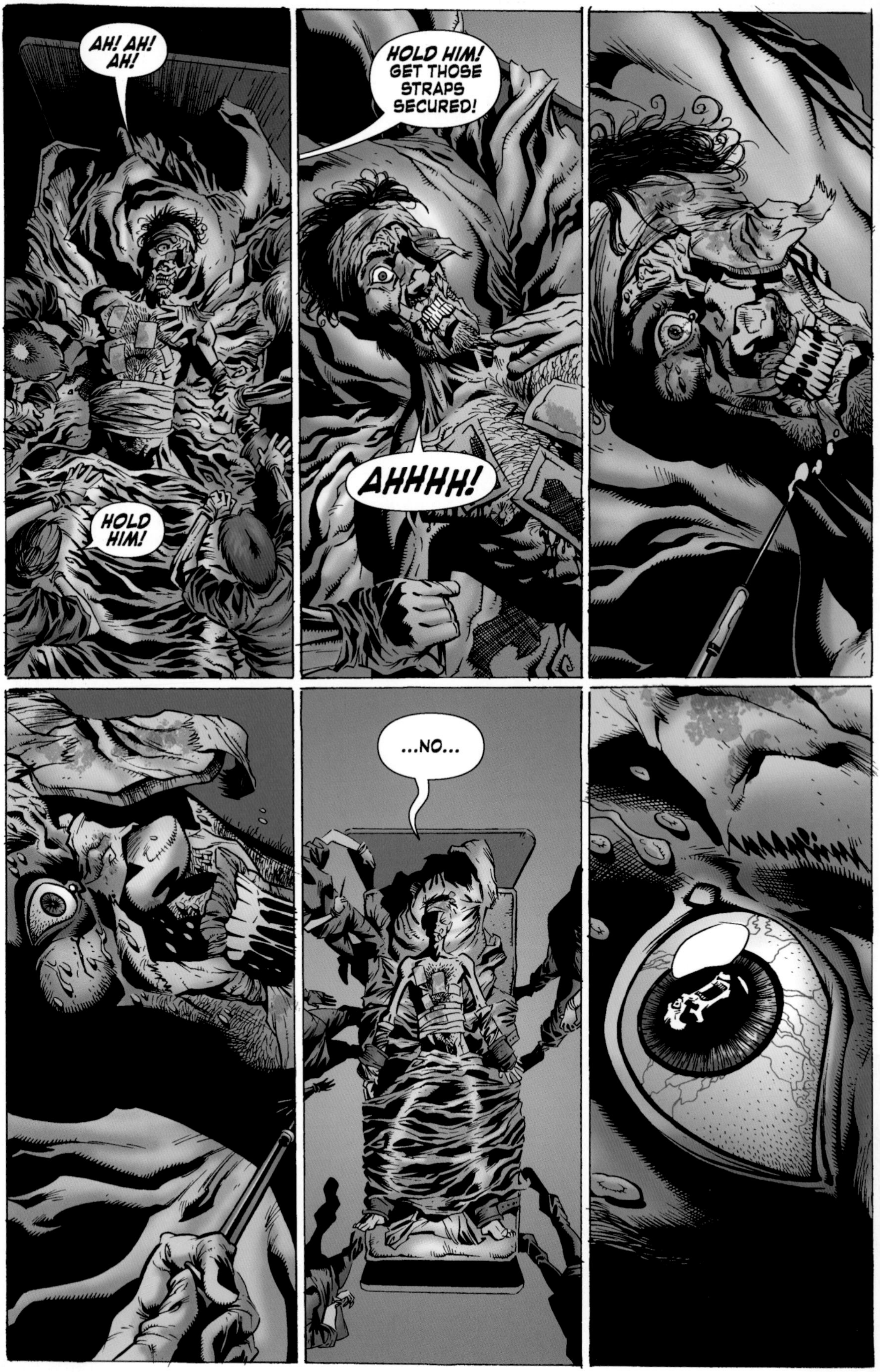
AH! AH! AH!
HOLD HIM!
HOLD HIM! GET THOSE STRAPS SECURED!
AHHHH!
...NO...

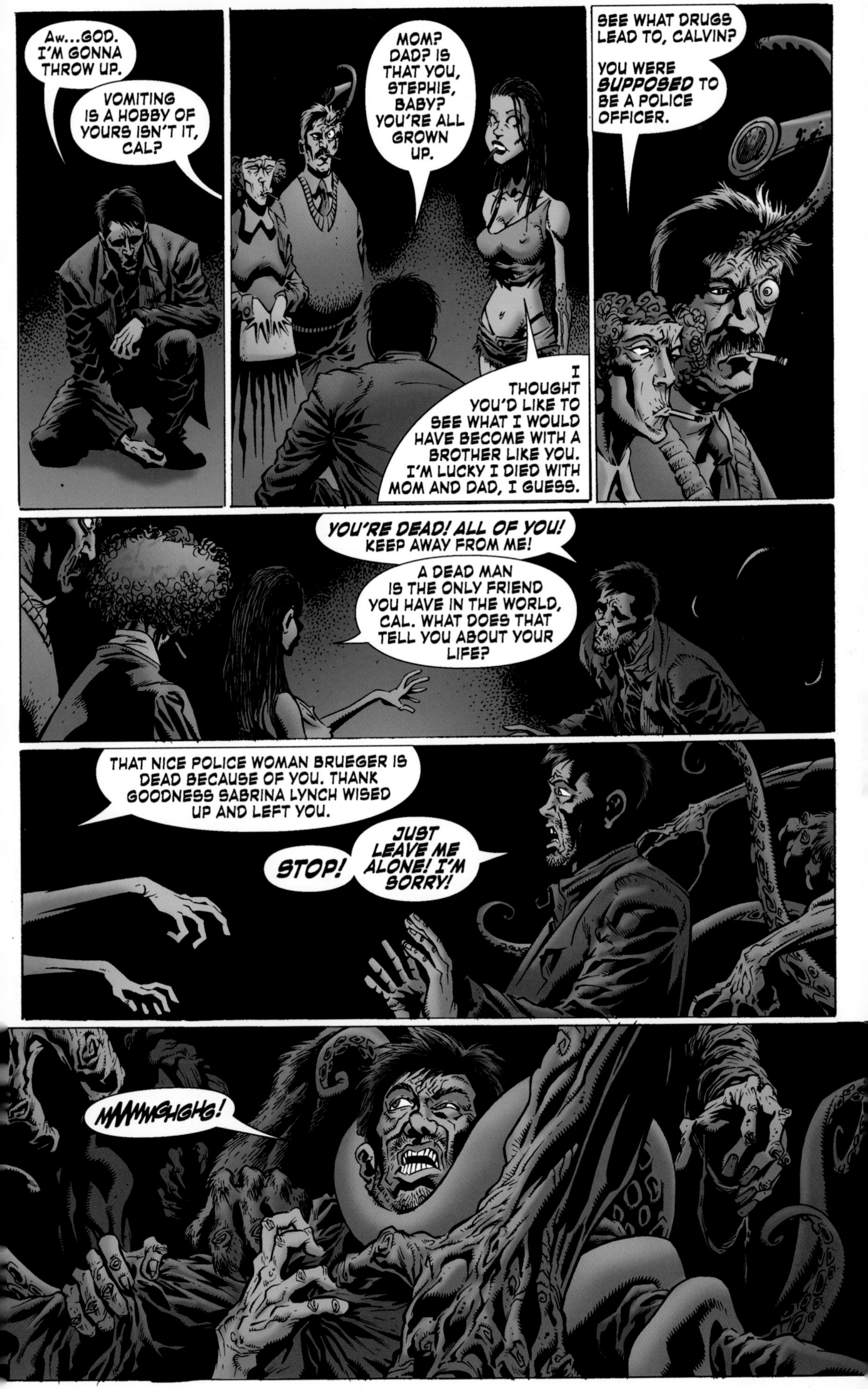
AW...GOD. I'M GONNA THROW UP.
VOMITING IS A HOBBY OF YOURS ISN'T IT, CAL?
MOM? DAD? IS THAT YOU, STEPHIE, BABY? YOU'RE ALL GROWN UP.
I THOUGHT YOU'D LIKE TO SEE WHAT I WOULD HAVE BECOME WITH A BROTHER LIKE YOU. I'M LUCKY I DIED WITH MOM AND DAD, I GUESS.
SEE WHAT DRUGS LEAD TO, CALVIN?
YOU WERE SUPPOSED TO BE A POLICE OFFICER.
YOU'RE DEAD! ALL OF YOU! KEEP AWAY FROM ME!
A DEAD MAN IS THE ONLY FRIEND YOU HAVE IN THE WORLD, CAL. WHAT DOES THAT TELL YOU ABOUT YOUR LIFE?
THAT NICE POLICE WOMAN BRUEGER IS DEAD BECAUSE OF YOU. THANK GOODNESS SABRINA LYNCH WISED UP AND LEFT YOU.
STOP!
JUST LEAVE ME ALONE! I'M SORRY!
MAAWMGHGHG!

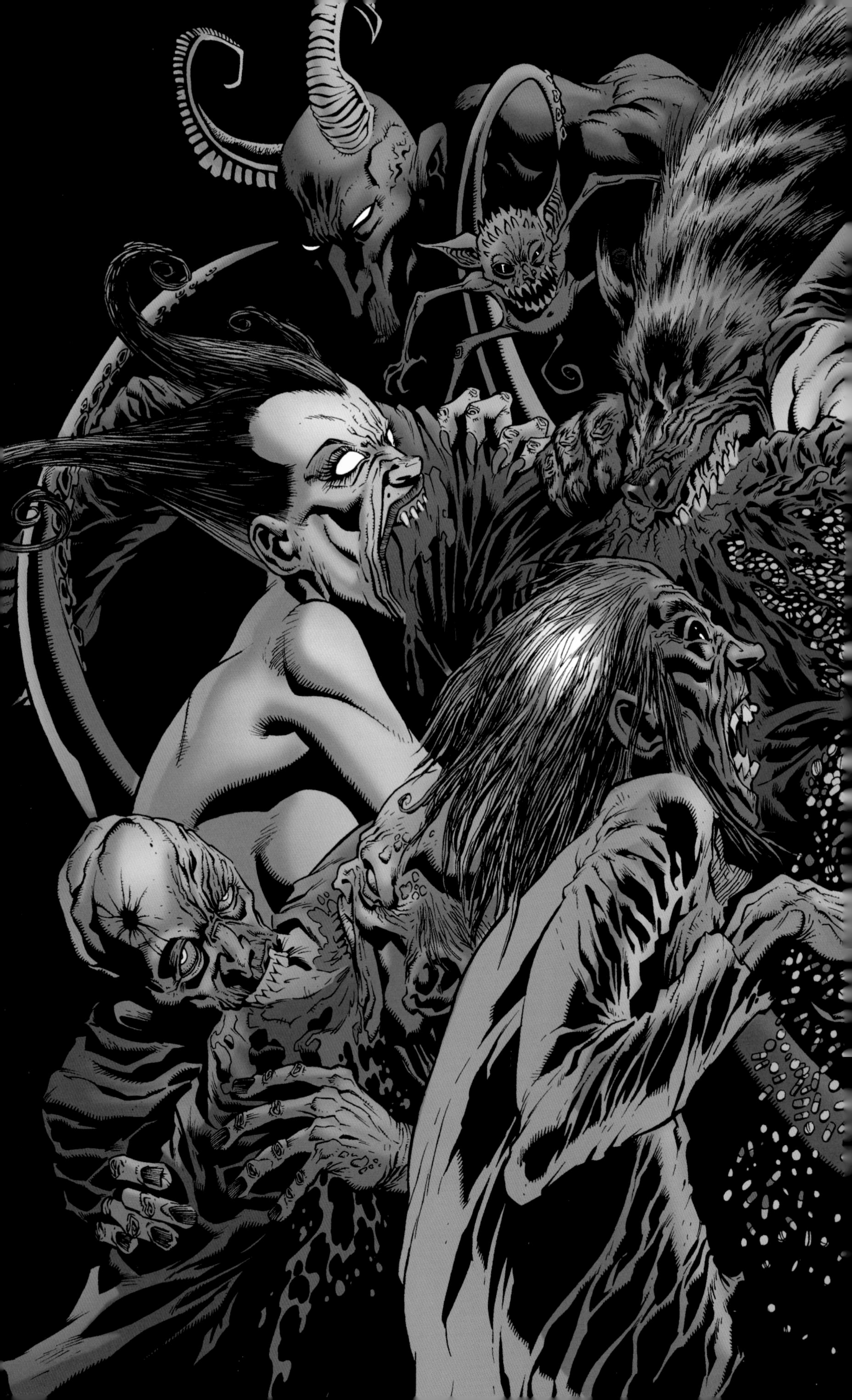

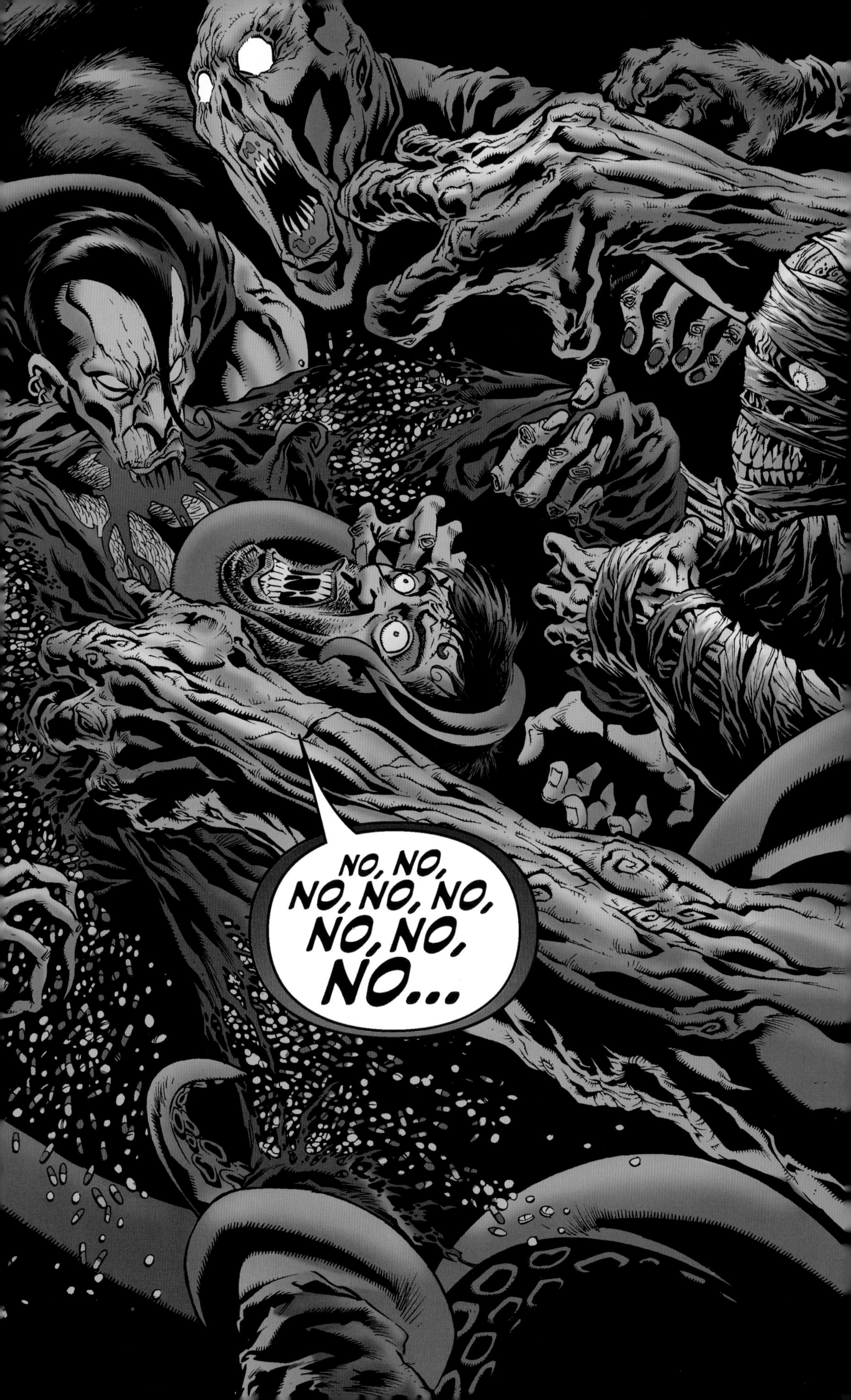
NO, NO, NO, NO, NO, NO, NO, NO...

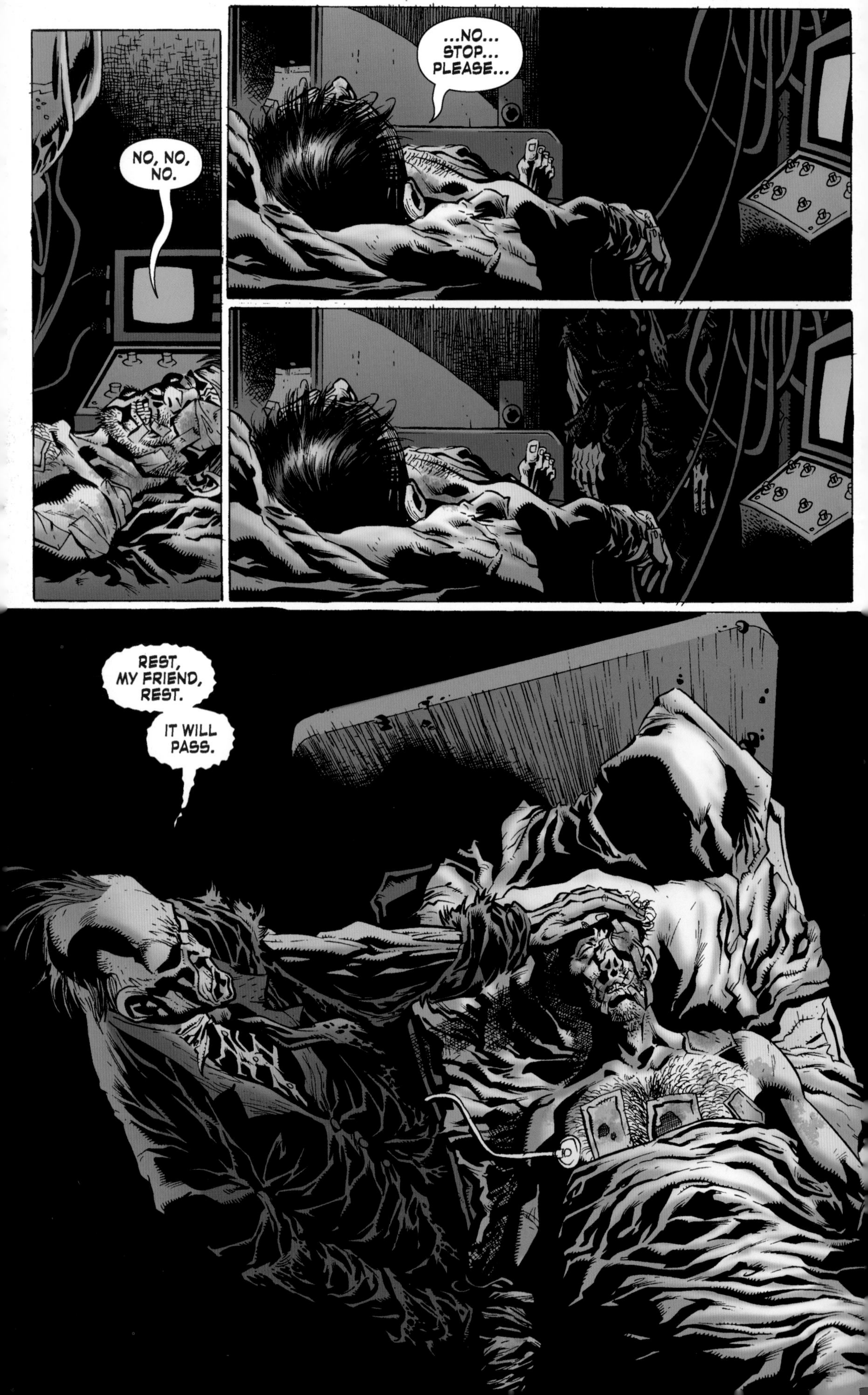
NO, NO, NO.
...NO... STOP... PLEASE...
REST, MY FRIEND, REST.
IT WILL PASS.

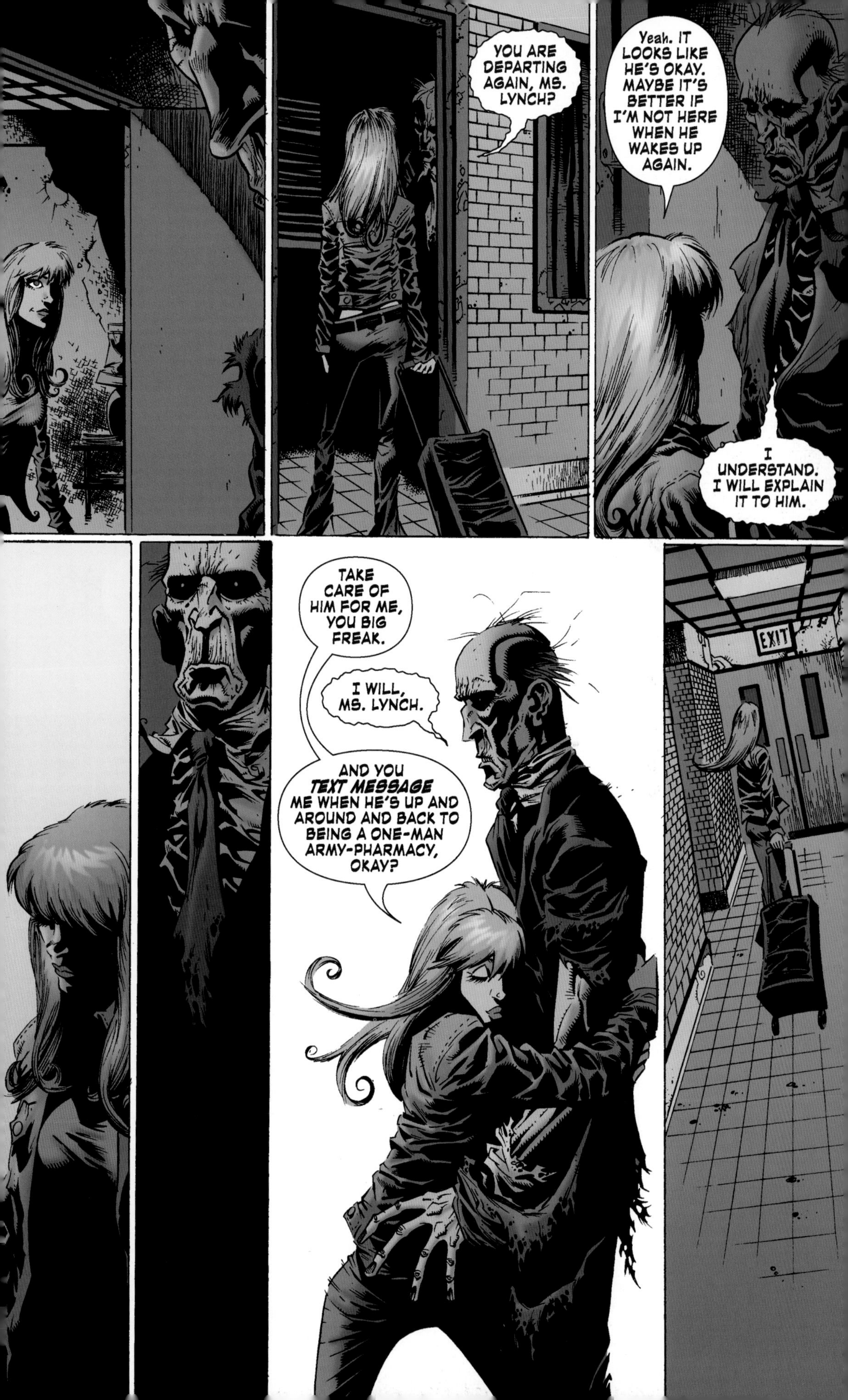
YOU ARE DEPARTING AGAIN, MS. LYNCH?
Yeah. IT LOOKS LIKE HE'S OKAY. MAYBE IT'S BETTER IF I'M NOT HERE WHEN HE WAKES UP AGAIN.
I UNDERSTAND. I WILL EXPLAIN IT TO HIM.
TAKE CARE OF HIM FOR ME, YOU BIG FREAK.
I WILL, MS. LYNCH.
AND YOU *TEXT MESSAGE* ME WHEN HE'S UP AND AROUND AND BACK TO BEING A ONE-MAN ARMY-PHARMACY, OKAY?
EXIT

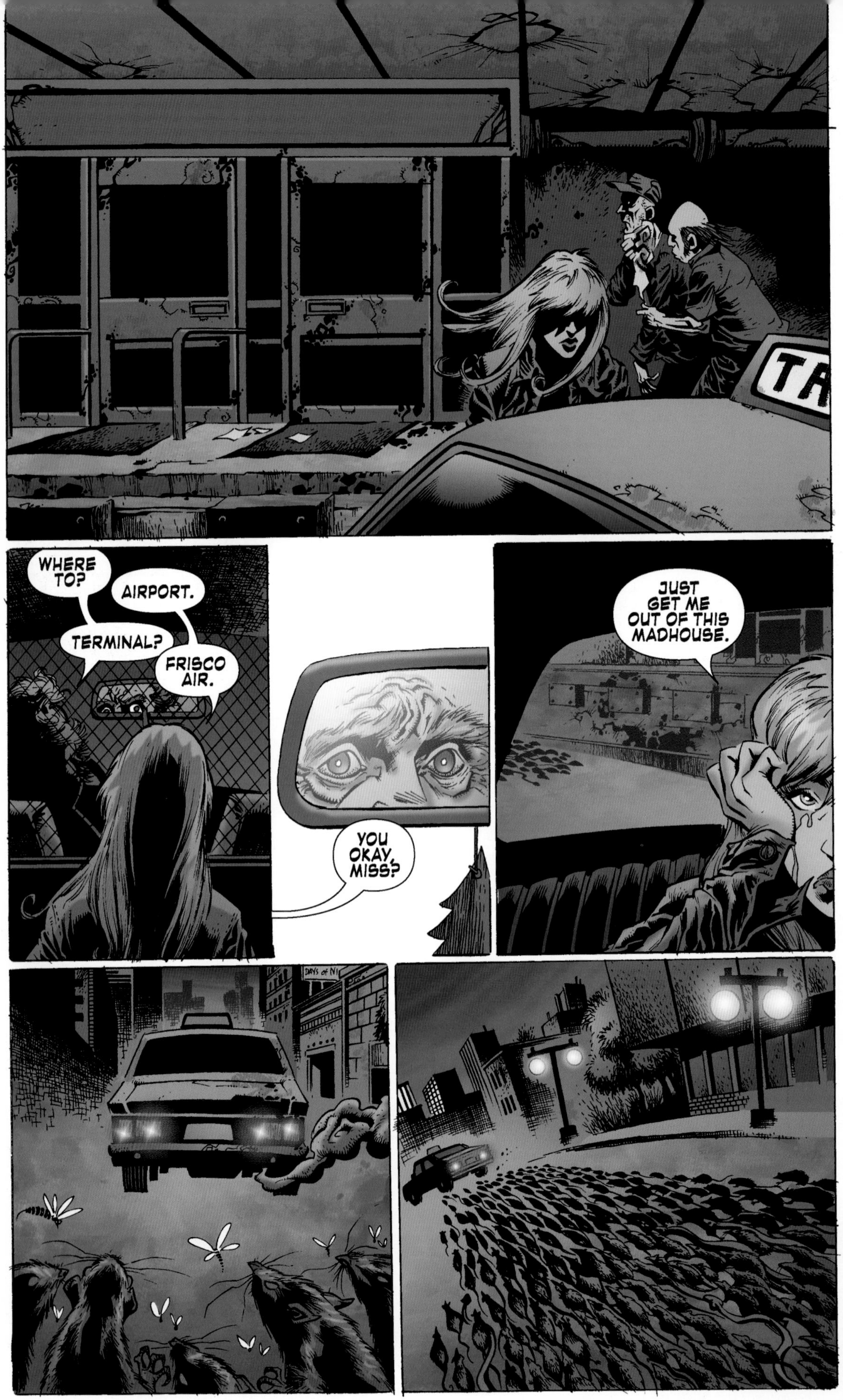
WHERE TO?
AIRPORT.
TERMINAL?
FRISCO AIR.
YOU OKAY, MISS?
JUST GET ME OUT OF THIS MADHOUSE.

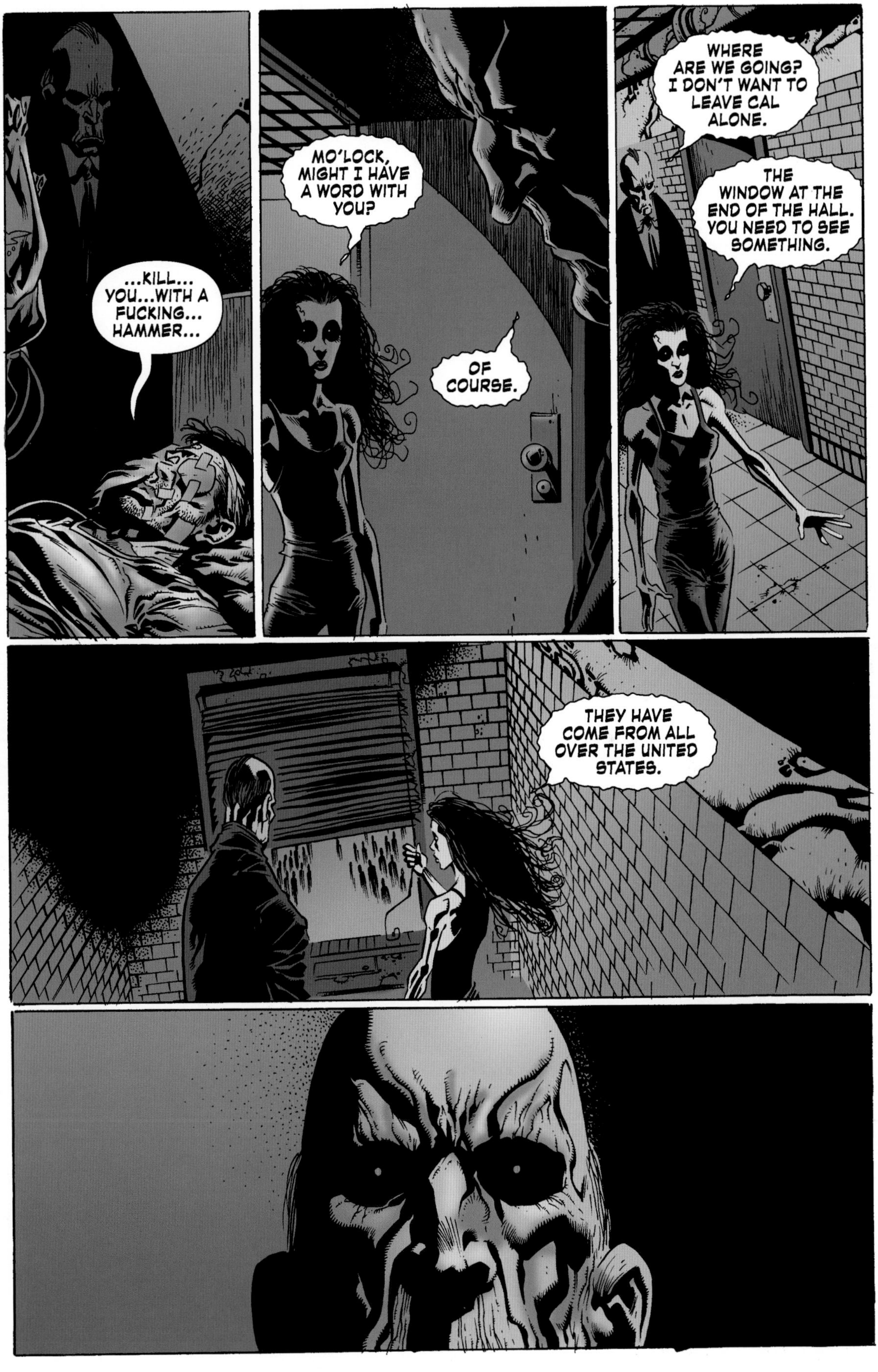
...KILL... YOU...WITH A FUCKING... HAMMER...
MO'LOCK, MIGHT I HAVE A WORD WITH YOU?
OF COURSE.
WHERE ARE WE GOING? I DON'T WANT TO LEAVE CAL ALONE.
THE WINDOW AT THE END OF THE HALL. YOU NEED TO SEE SOMETHING.
THEY HAVE COME FROM ALL OVER THE UNITED STATES.

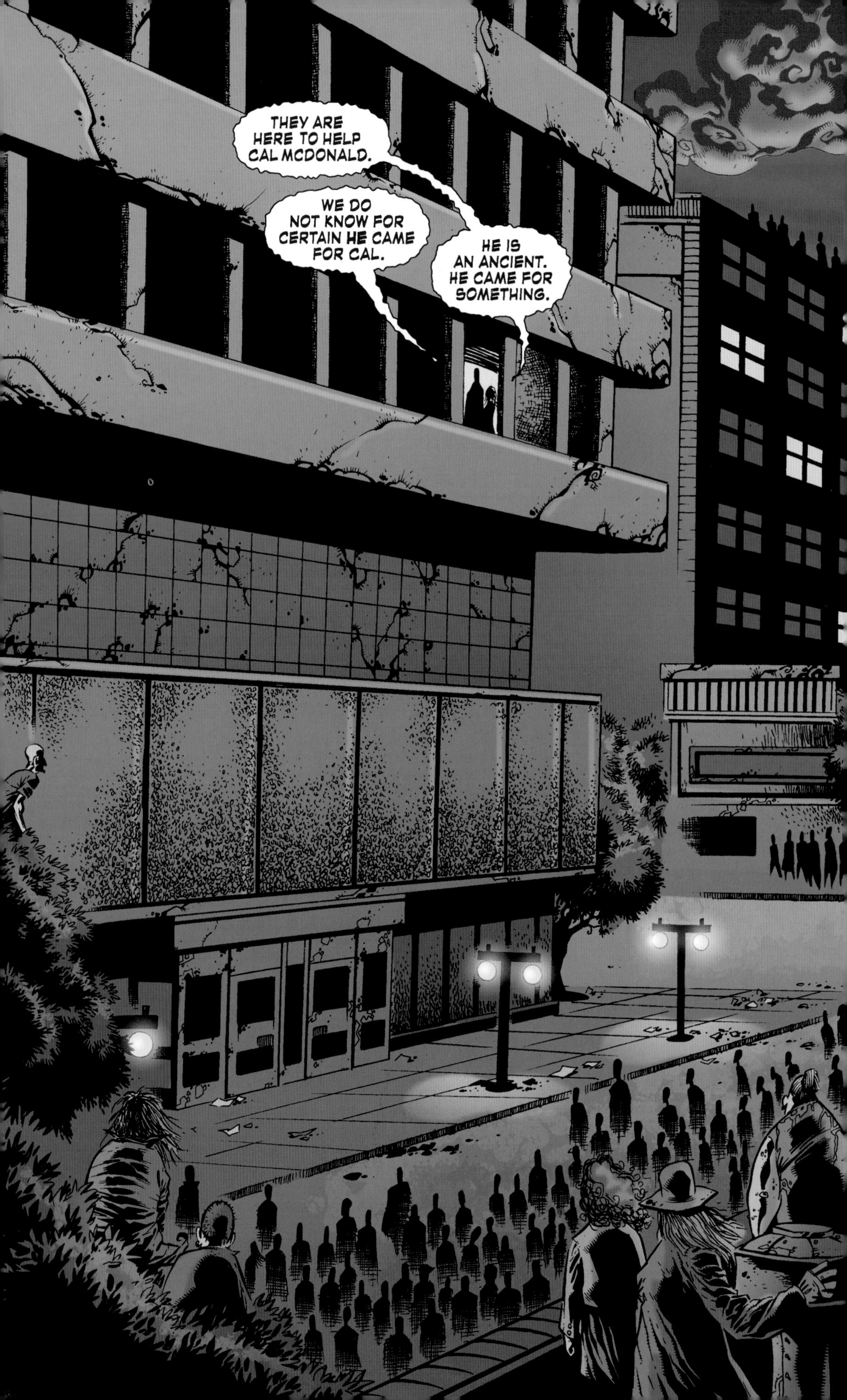
THEY ARE HERE TO HELP CAL MCDONALD.
WE DO NOT KNOW FOR CERTAIN HE CAME FOR CAL.
HE IS AN ANCIENT. HE CAME FOR SOMETHING.

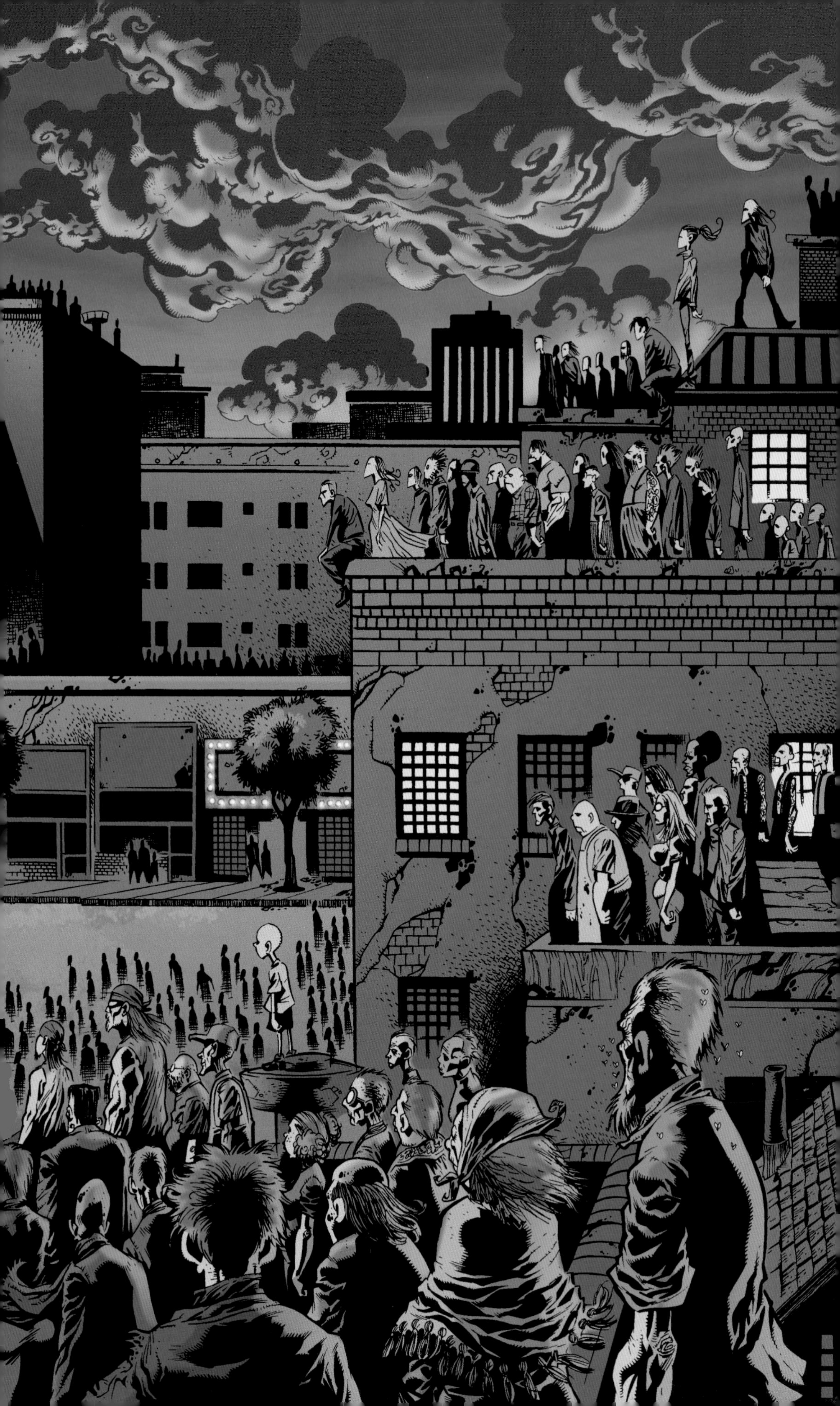

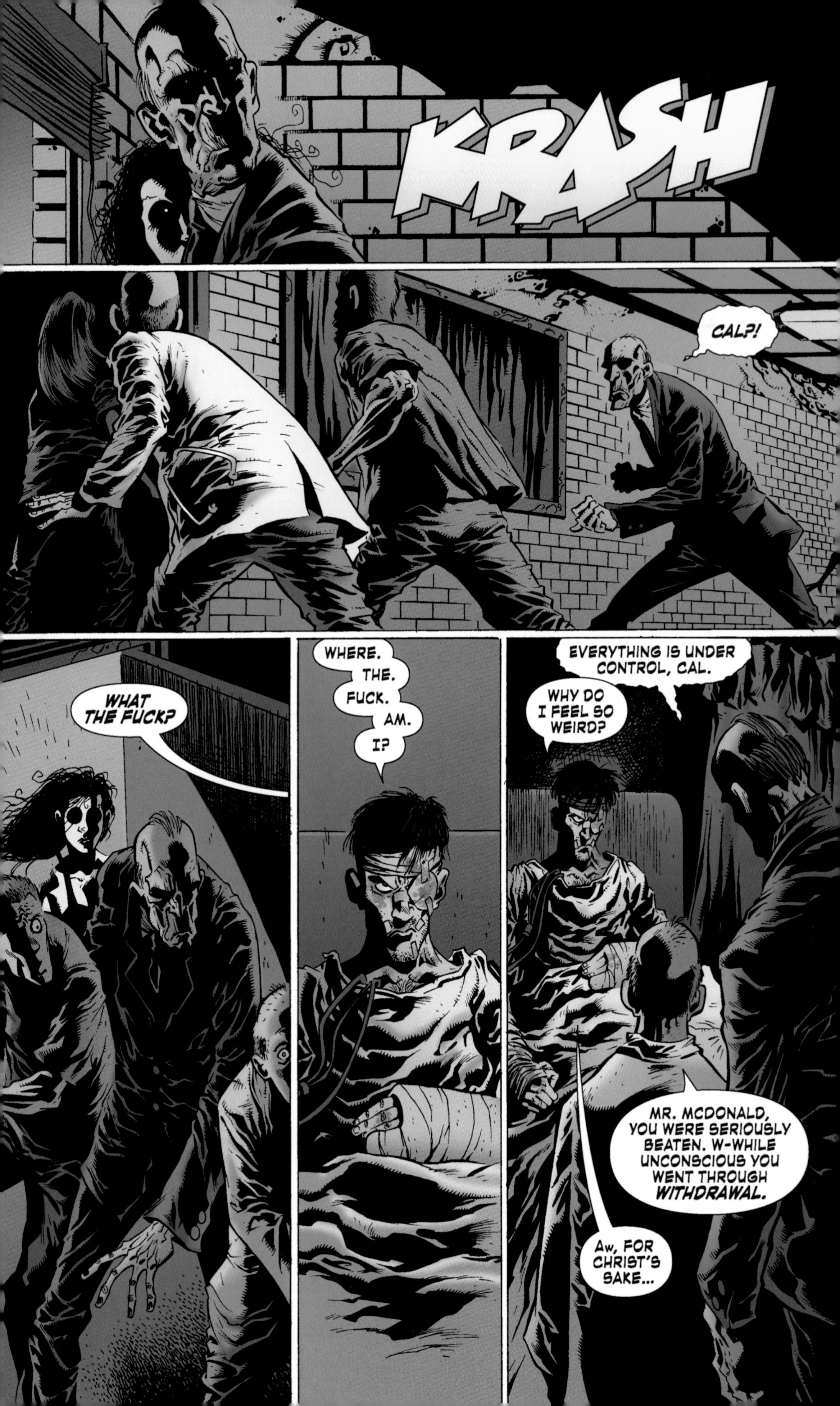
KRASH
CAL?!
WHAT THE FUCK?
WHERE. THE. FUCK. AM. I?
EVERYTHING IS UNDER CONTROL, CAL.
WHY DO I FEEL SO WEIRD?
MR. MCDONALD, YOU WERE SERIOUSLY BEATEN. W-WHILE UNCONSCIOUS YOU WENT THROUGH *WITHDRAWAL.*
Aw, FOR CHRIST'S SAKE...

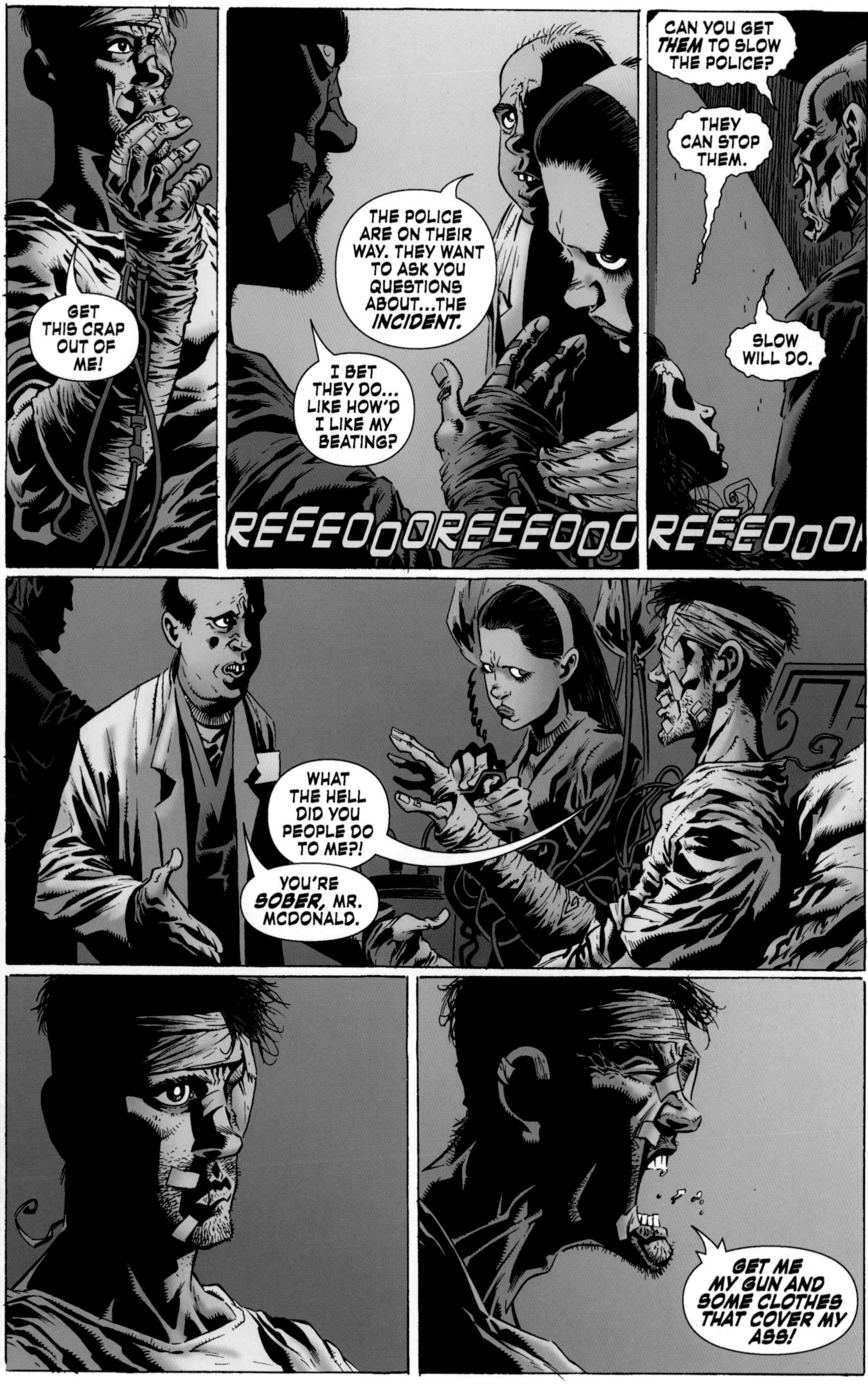

GET THIS CRAP OUT OF ME!
THE POLICE ARE ON THEIR WAY. THEY WANT TO ASK YOU QUESTIONS ABOUT...THE *INCIDENT.*
I BET THEY DO... LIKE HOW'D I LIKE MY BEATING?
REEEOOOOREEEEOOO
CAN YOU GET *THEM* TO SLOW THE POLICE?
THEY CAN STOP THEM.
SLOW WILL DO.
REEEEOOOO
WHAT THE HELL DID YOU PEOPLE DO TO ME?!
YOU'RE *SOBER,* MR. MCDONALD.
GET ME MY GUN AND SOME CLOTHES THAT COVER MY ASS!

I THOUGHT SABRINA WAS HERE?

CAL... SABRINA HAD TO LEAVE. YOU COULD CALL--

SHE LEFT? I CAN'T TALK TO HER.

SHE WANTED YOU TO TEXT MESSAGE HER... SHE'D RATHER NOT SPEAK, I ASSUME.

TEXT MESSAGING IS FOR GIRLS.

AND GHOULS.

DON'T MAKE ME SHOOT YOU.

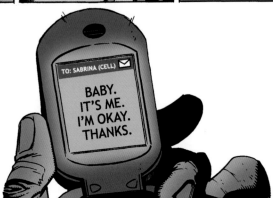

TO: SABRINA (CELL)

BABY. IT'S ME. I'M OKAY. THANKS.

MAYBE YOU FUCKS DIDN'T HEAR ME BEFORE...GET ME MY GUN AND SOME CLOTHES THAT COVER MY ASS!

MY BRETHREN HAVE COME FROM ALL OVER TO HELP. THEY ARE HOLDING THE POLICE AT BAY, BUT THEY CANNOT DO IT LONG. A GREAT EVIL HAS COME TO LOS ANGELES. I SHOULD HAVE TOLD YOU SOONER.

ALL RIGHT. GET MY SHIT.

BADEEP BADEEP

THAT IS PROBABLY MS. SABRINA RETURNING YOUR MESSAGE.

BADEEP BADEEP

Yeah, PROBABLY WITH A "FUCK YOU" SMILIE.

CAL... WHAT IS IT?

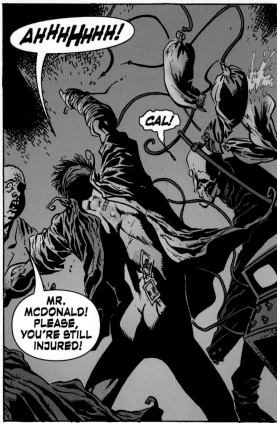

AHHHHHHH!

CAL!

MR. MCDONALD! PLEASE, YOU'RE STILL INJURED!

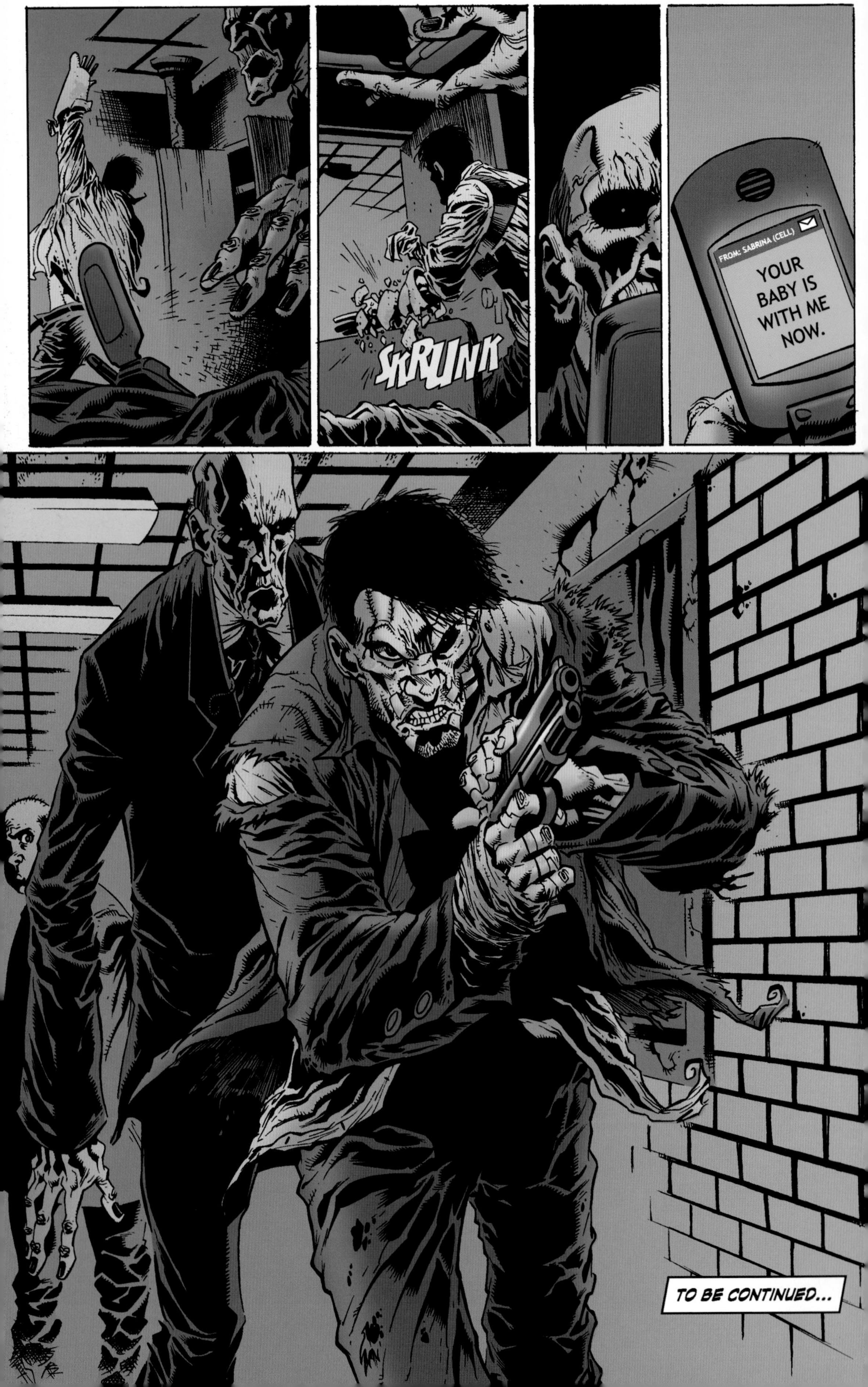
SKRUNK
FROM: SABRINA (CELL)
YOUR BABY IS WITH ME NOW.
TO BE CONTINUED...

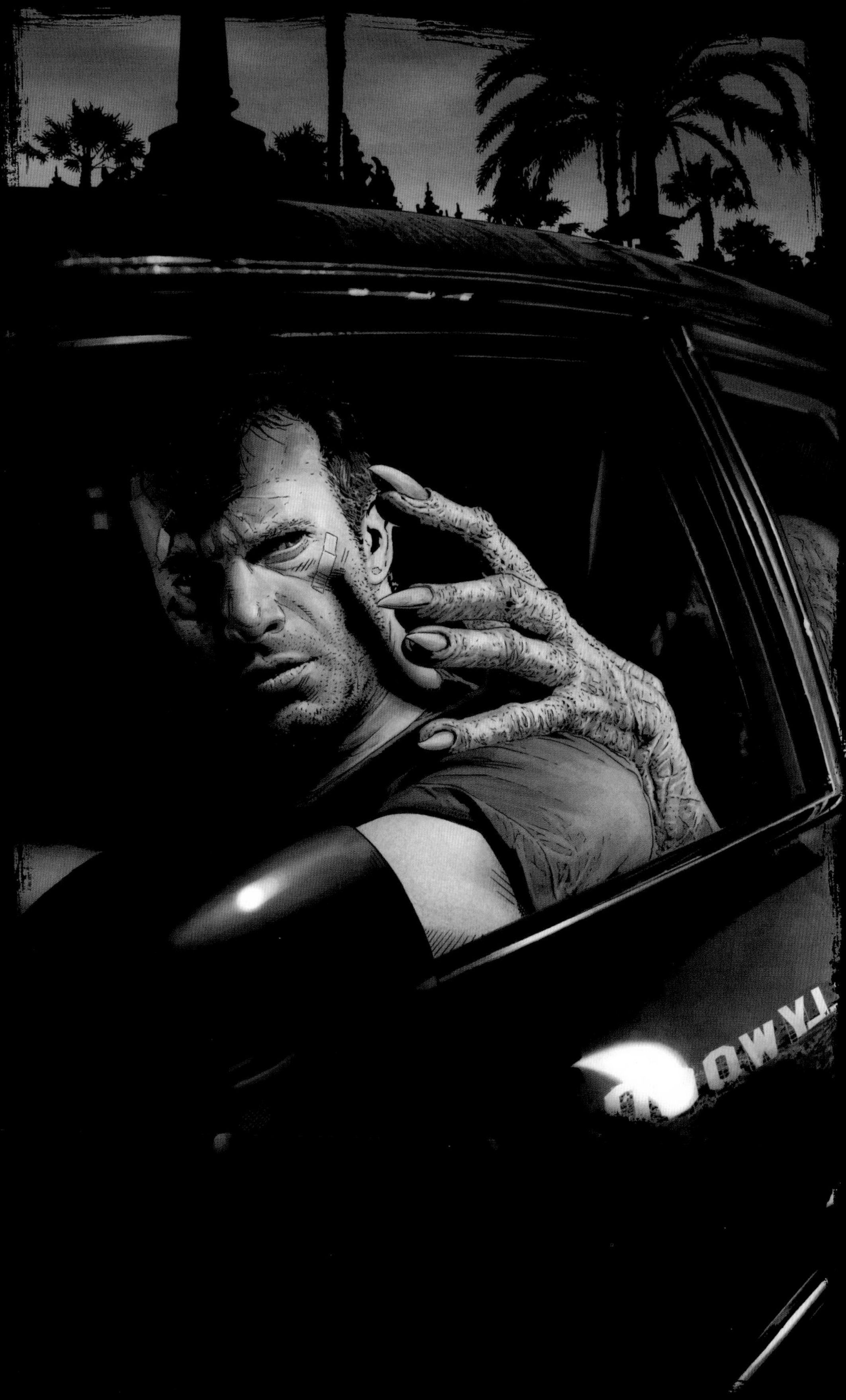

CHAPTER THREE

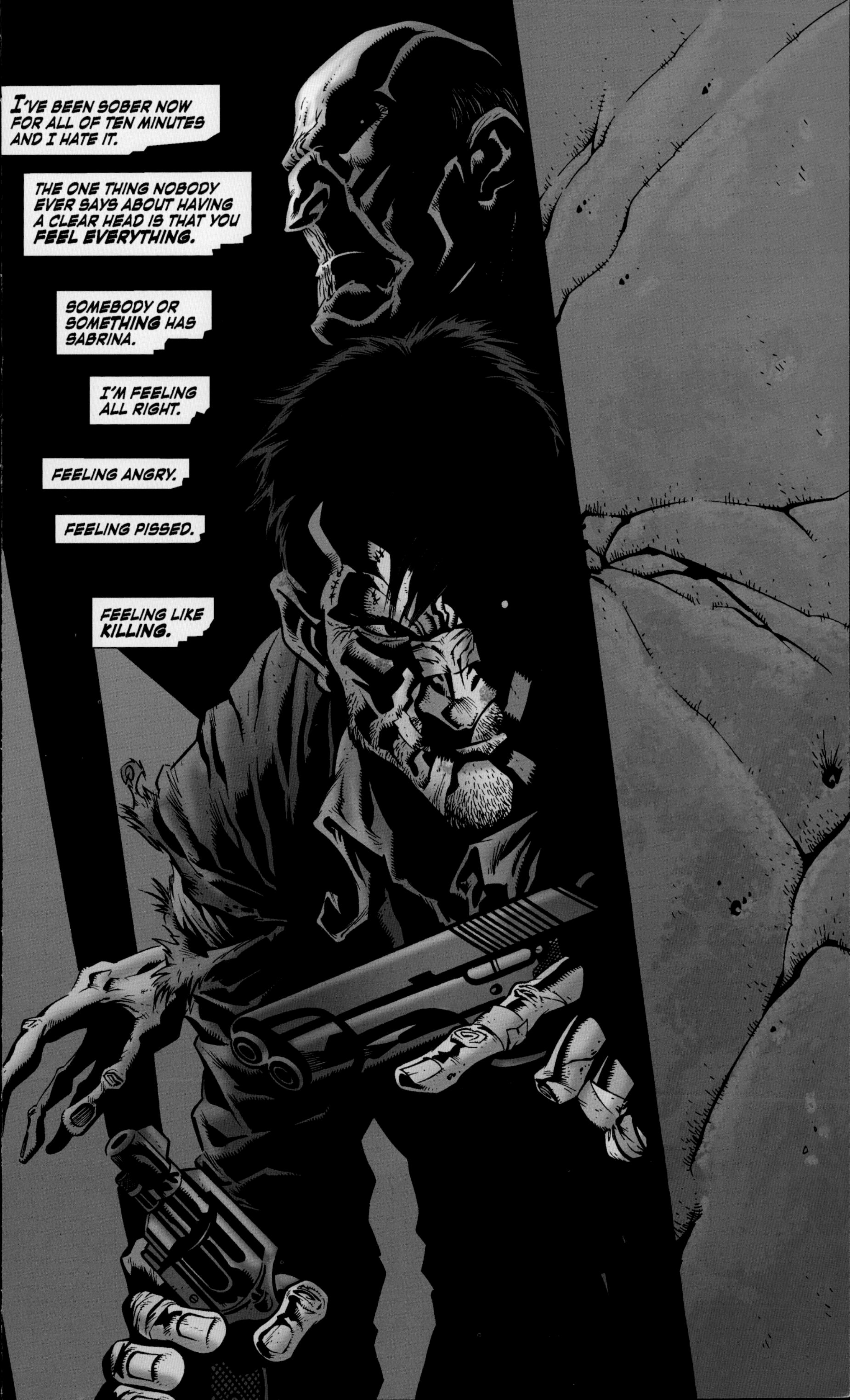
I'VE BEEN SOBER NOW FOR ALL OF TEN MINUTES AND I HATE IT.
THE ONE THING NOBODY EVER SAYS ABOUT HAVING A CLEAR HEAD IS THAT YOU FEEL EVERYTHING.
SOMEBODY OR SOMETHING HAS SABRINA.
I'M FEELING ALL RIGHT.
FEELING ANGRY.
FEELING PISSED.
FEELING LIKE KILLING.

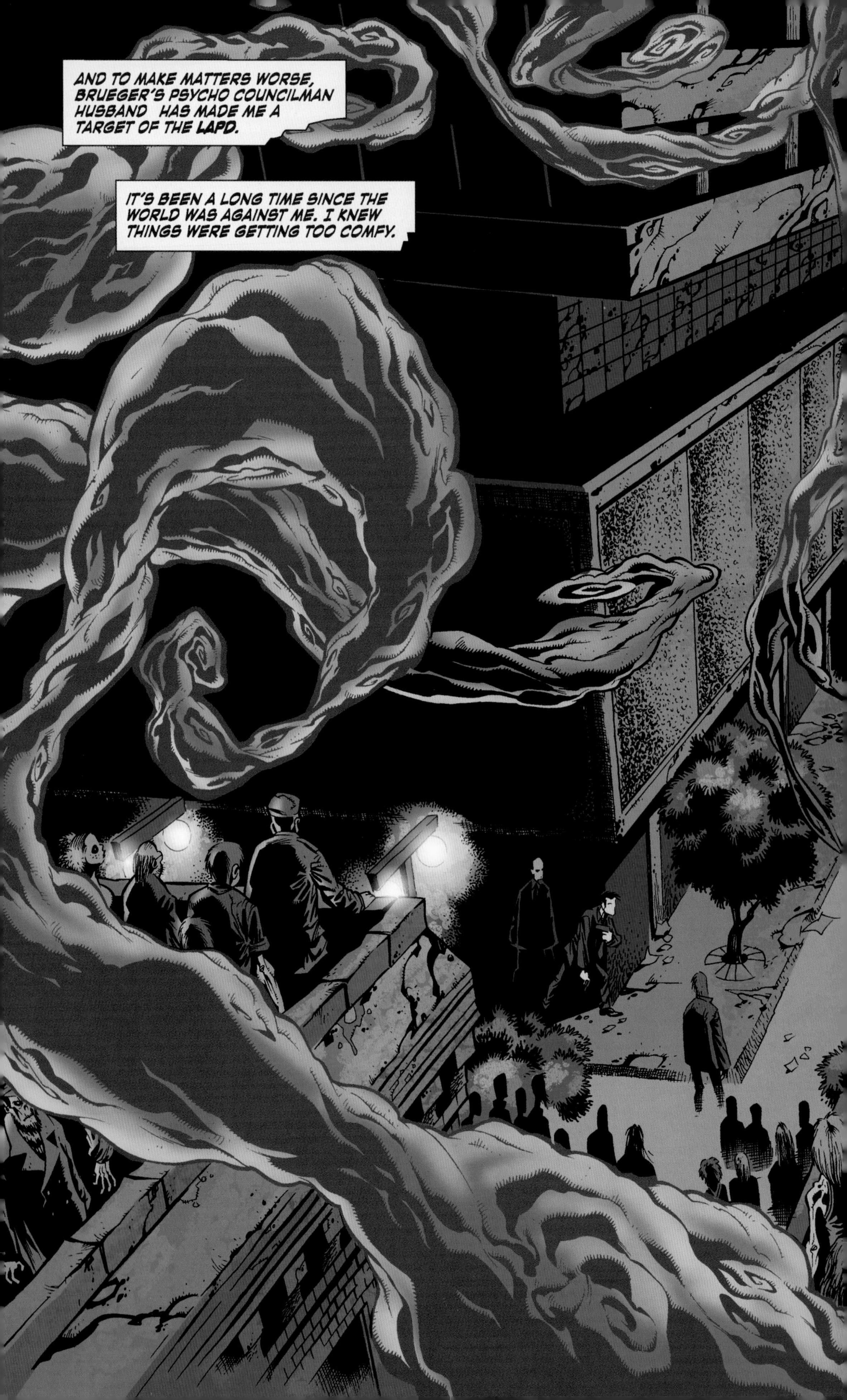
AND TO MAKE MATTERS WORSE, BRUEGER'S PSYCHO COUNCILMAN HUSBAND HAS MADE ME A TARGET OF THE LAPD.
IT'S BEEN A LONG TIME SINCE THE WORLD WAS AGAINST ME. I KNEW THINGS WERE GETTING TOO COMFY.

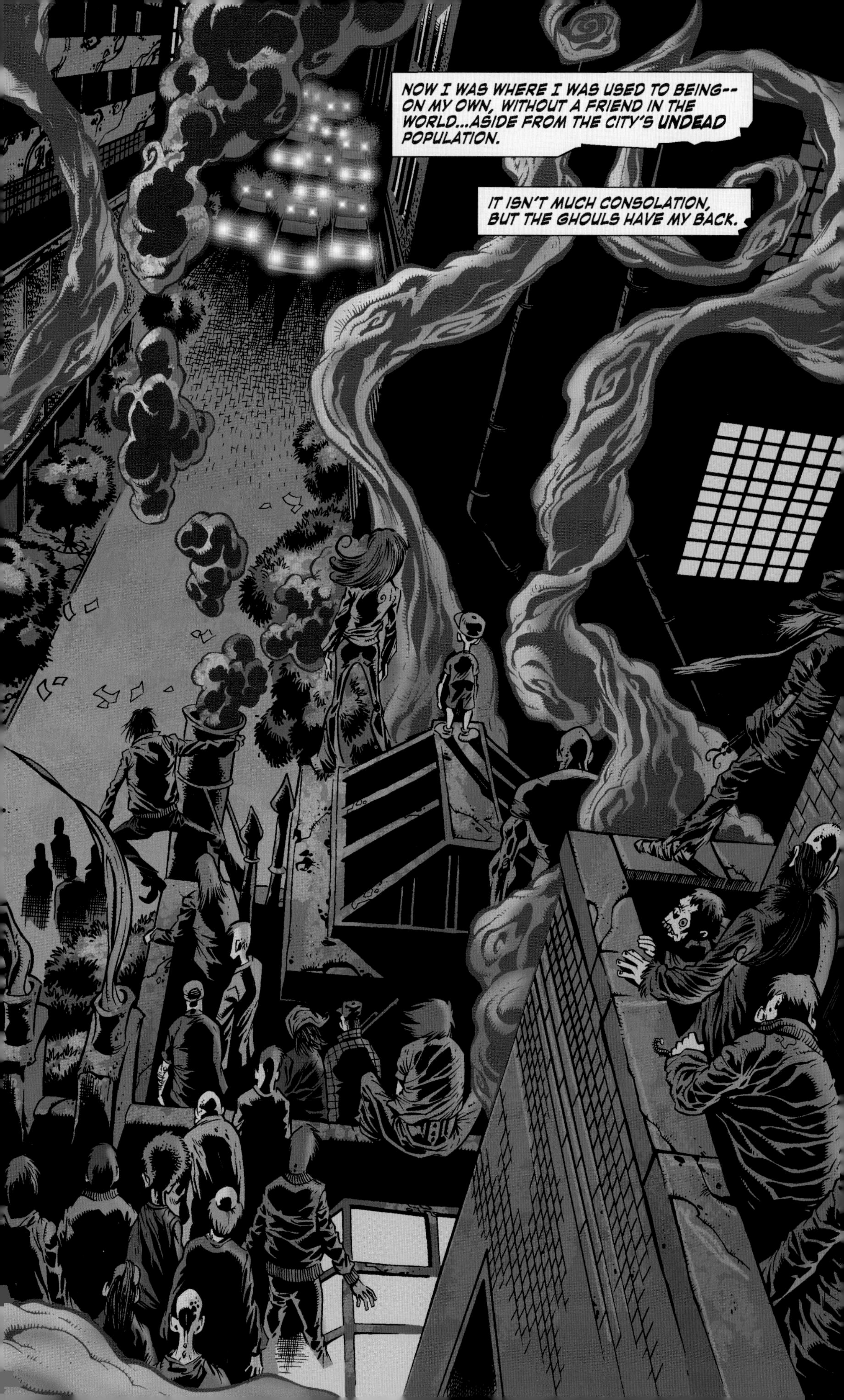
NOW I WAS WHERE I WAS USED TO BEING-- ON MY OWN, WITHOUT A FRIEND IN THE WORLD...ASIDE FROM THE CITY'S UNDEAD POPULATION.
IT ISN'T MUCH CONSOLATION, BUT THE GHOULS HAVE MY BACK.

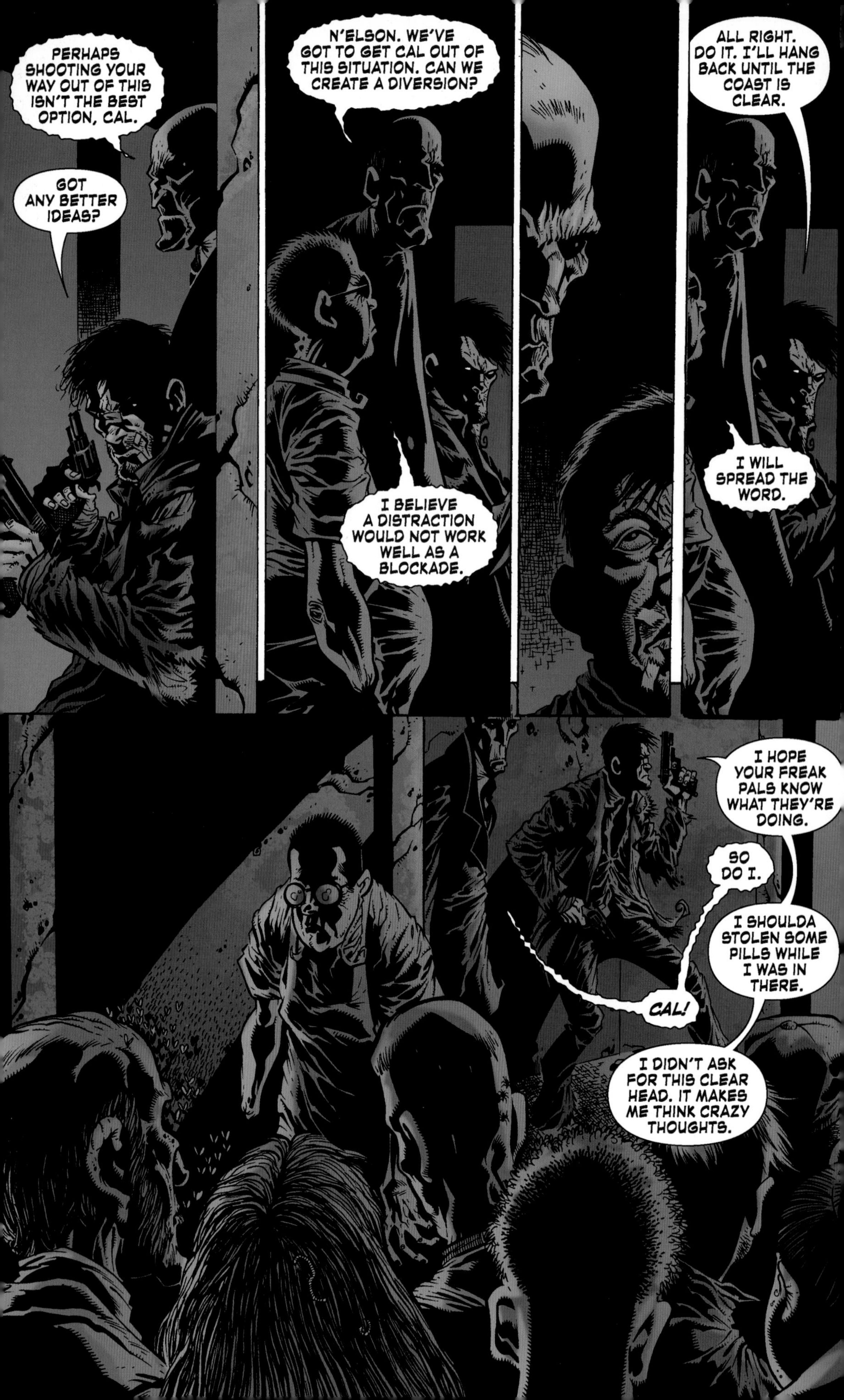
PERHAPS SHOOTING YOUR WAY OUT OF THIS ISN'T THE BEST OPTION, CAL.
GOT ANY BETTER IDEAS?
N'ELSON. WE'VE GOT TO GET CAL OUT OF THIS SITUATION. CAN WE CREATE A DIVERSION?
I BELIEVE A DISTRACTION WOULD NOT WORK WELL AS A BLOCKADE.
ALL RIGHT. DO IT. I'LL HANG BACK UNTIL THE COAST IS CLEAR.
I WILL SPREAD THE WORD.
I HOPE YOUR FREAK PALS KNOW WHAT THEY'RE DOING.
SO DO I.
I SHOULDA STOLEN SOME PILLS WHILE I WAS IN THERE.
CAL!
I DIDN'T ASK FOR THIS CLEAR HEAD. IT MAKES ME THINK CRAZY THOUGHTS.

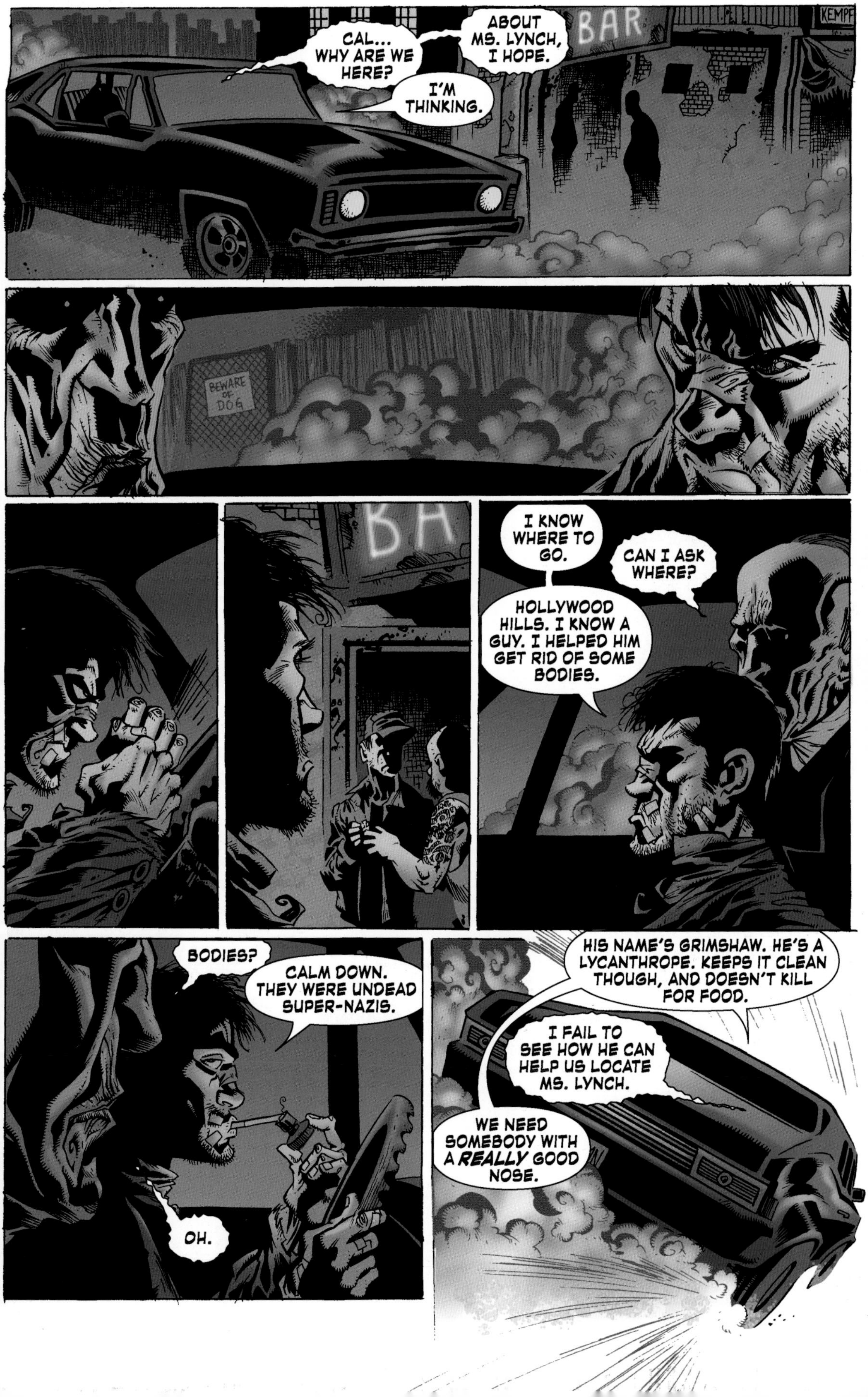
BAR
KEMPF
CAL... WHY ARE WE HERE?
ABOUT MS. LYNCH, I HOPE.
I'M THINKING.
BEWARE OF DOG
I KNOW WHERE TO GO.
CAN I ASK WHERE?
HOLLYWOOD HILLS. I KNOW A GUY. I HELPED HIM GET RID OF SOME BODIES.
BODIES?
CALM DOWN. THEY WERE UNDEAD SUPER-NAZIS.
OH.
HIS NAME'S GRIMSHAW. HE'S A LYCANTHROPE. KEEPS IT CLEAN THOUGH, AND DOESN'T KILL FOR FOOD.
I FAIL TO SEE HOW HE CAN HELP US LOCATE MS. LYNCH.
WE NEED SOMEBODY WITH A *REALLY* GOOD NOSE.

WHO WAS I KIDDING? I COULD HARDLY THINK. I HATED MYSELF FOR THINKING ABOUT SOMETHING TO NUMB ME. SOMETHING TO BLUR MY MIND.

I CAN'T EVEN DESCRIBE THE FEELING IN MY GUT. IT WAS LIKE A GLASS-SPIKED STONE HAD BEEN LAID TO REST IN MY BELLY.

IT WASN'T SOME LAME-ASS DRUG CRAVING PAIN EITHER. THOSE WERE ALL IN MY HEAD.

IT WAS KNOWING THAT EVERY SECOND THAT WENT BY MADE IT LESS LIKELY WE'D FIND SABRINA ALIVE.

IF AT ALL.

ON THE WAY TO GRIMSHAW'S PLACE IN THE HOLLYWOOD HILLS, MO'LOCK SPREAD THE WORD ABOUT SABRINA TO THE GHOULS.

AND BROTHER, PLEASE REMEMBER THE FREIGHT SHIP THAT CRASHED INTO SANTA MONICA PIER. ITS OCCUPANT WAS MOST SUSPICIOUS.

WHAT FREIGHTER?

I HAVE TO GO. SPREAD THE WORD, BROTHER.

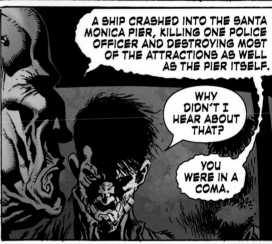

A SHIP CRASHED INTO THE SANTA MONICA PIER, KILLING ONE POLICE OFFICER AND DESTROYING MOST OF THE ATTRACTIONS AS WELL AS THE PIER ITSELF.

WHY DIDN'T I HEAR ABOUT THAT?

YOU WERE IN A COMA.

IS WHAT HAPPENED WORTH MENTIONING TO YOUR FREAK-ASS FRIENDS?

THEY ARE YOUR FRIENDS TOO, CAL. THEY CARE ABOUT YOU.

SHUT UP.

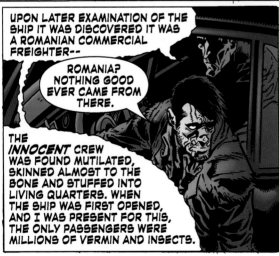

UPON LATER EXAMINATION OF THE SHIP IT WAS DISCOVERED IT WAS A ROMANIAN COMMERCIAL FREIGHTER--

ROMANIA? NOTHING GOOD EVER CAME FROM THERE.

THE *INNOCENT* CREW WAS FOUND MUTILATED, SKINNED ALMOST TO THE BONE AND STUFFED INTO LIVING QUARTERS. WHEN THE SHIP WAS FIRST OPENED, AND I WAS PRESENT FOR THIS, THE ONLY PASSENGERS WERE MILLIONS OF VERMIN AND INSECTS.

I SAW THE RATS FORM INTO WHAT APPEARED TO BE AN ANCIENT UNDEAD...FROM THE OLD COUNTRY. IF I VENTURED TO GUESS I'D SAY HE WAS ONE OF THE ORIGINALS.

OLD WORLD VAMPIRE. FUCKIN' GREAT.

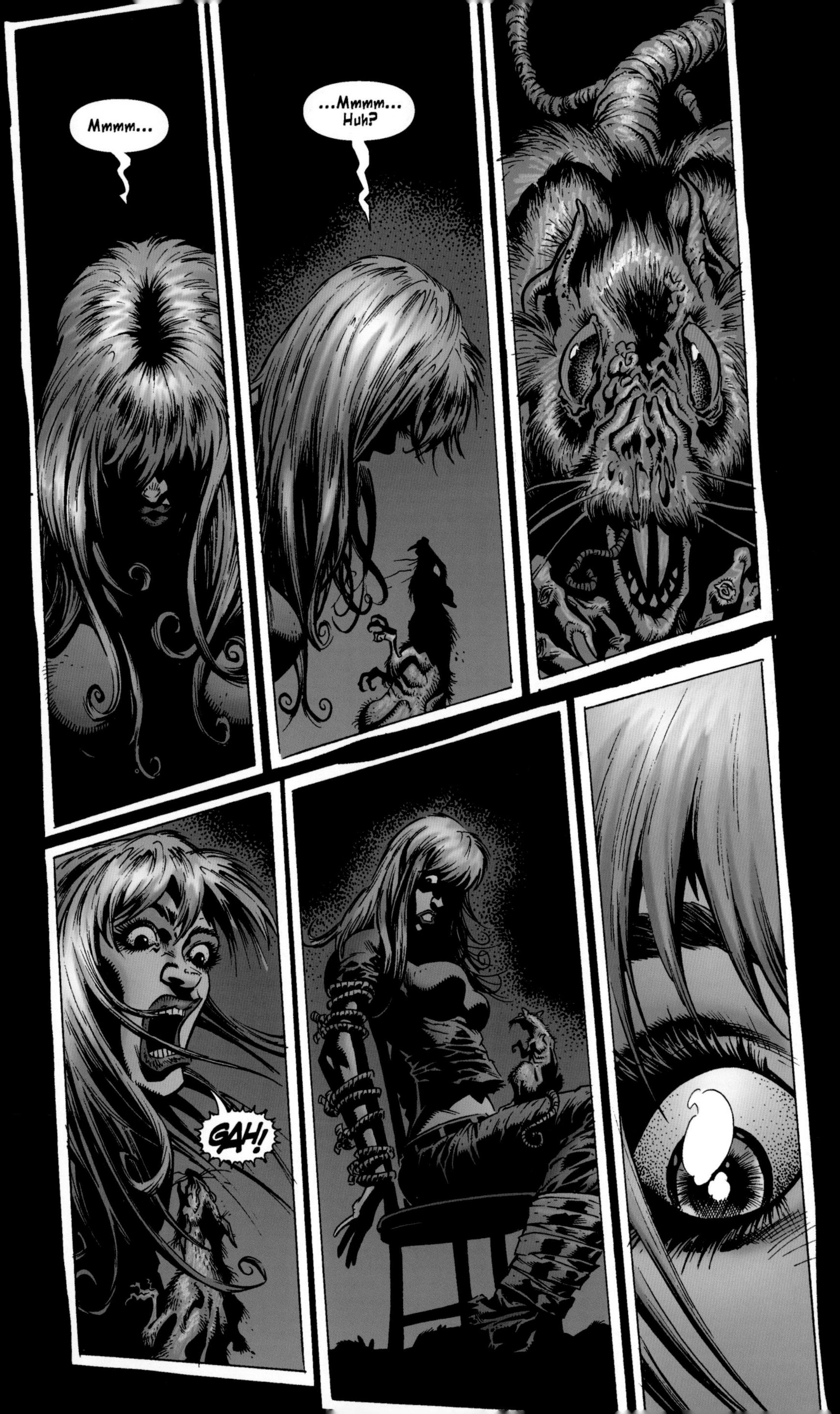
Mmmm...
...Mmmm...
Huh?
GAH!

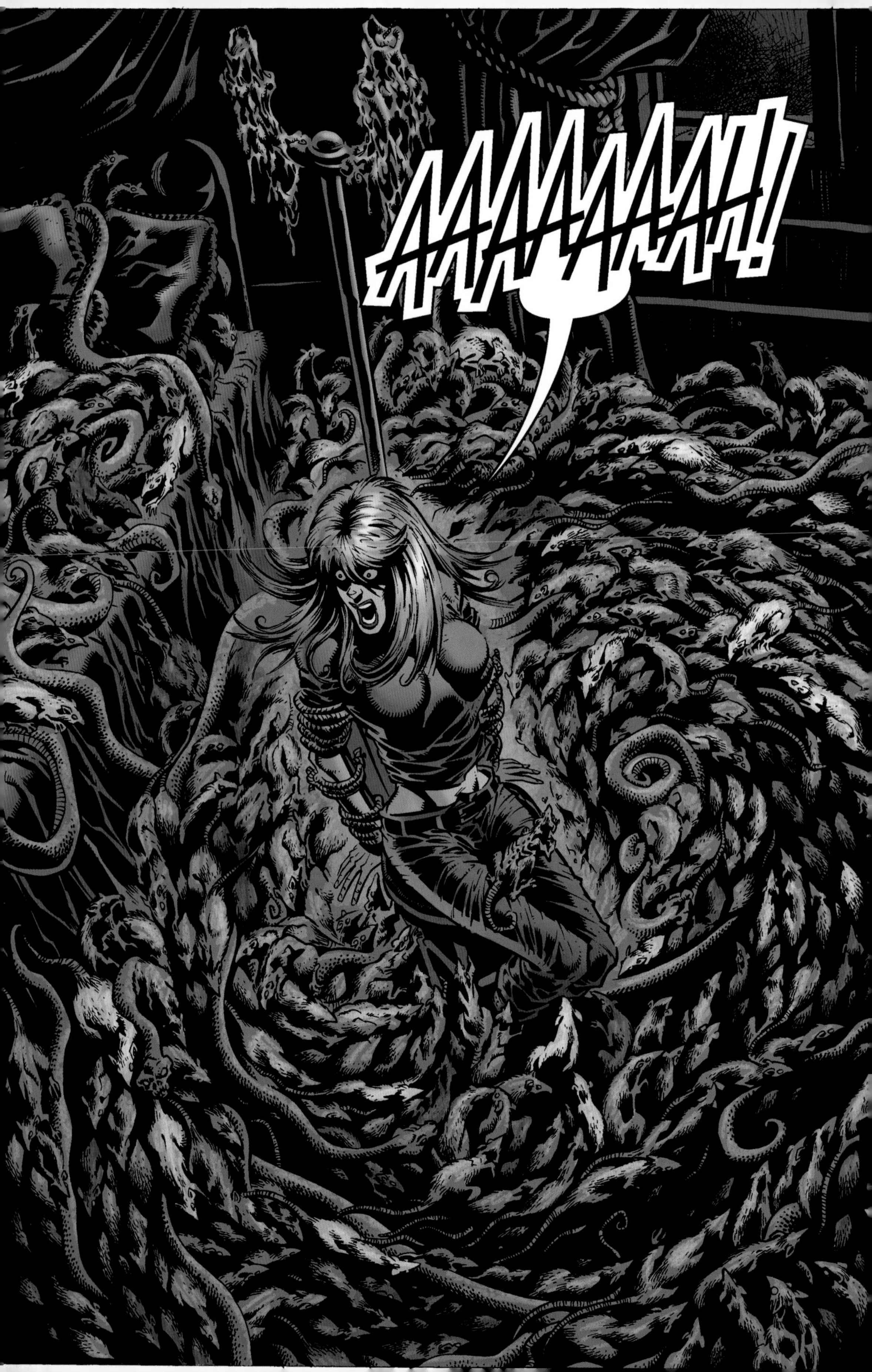
AAAAAAH!

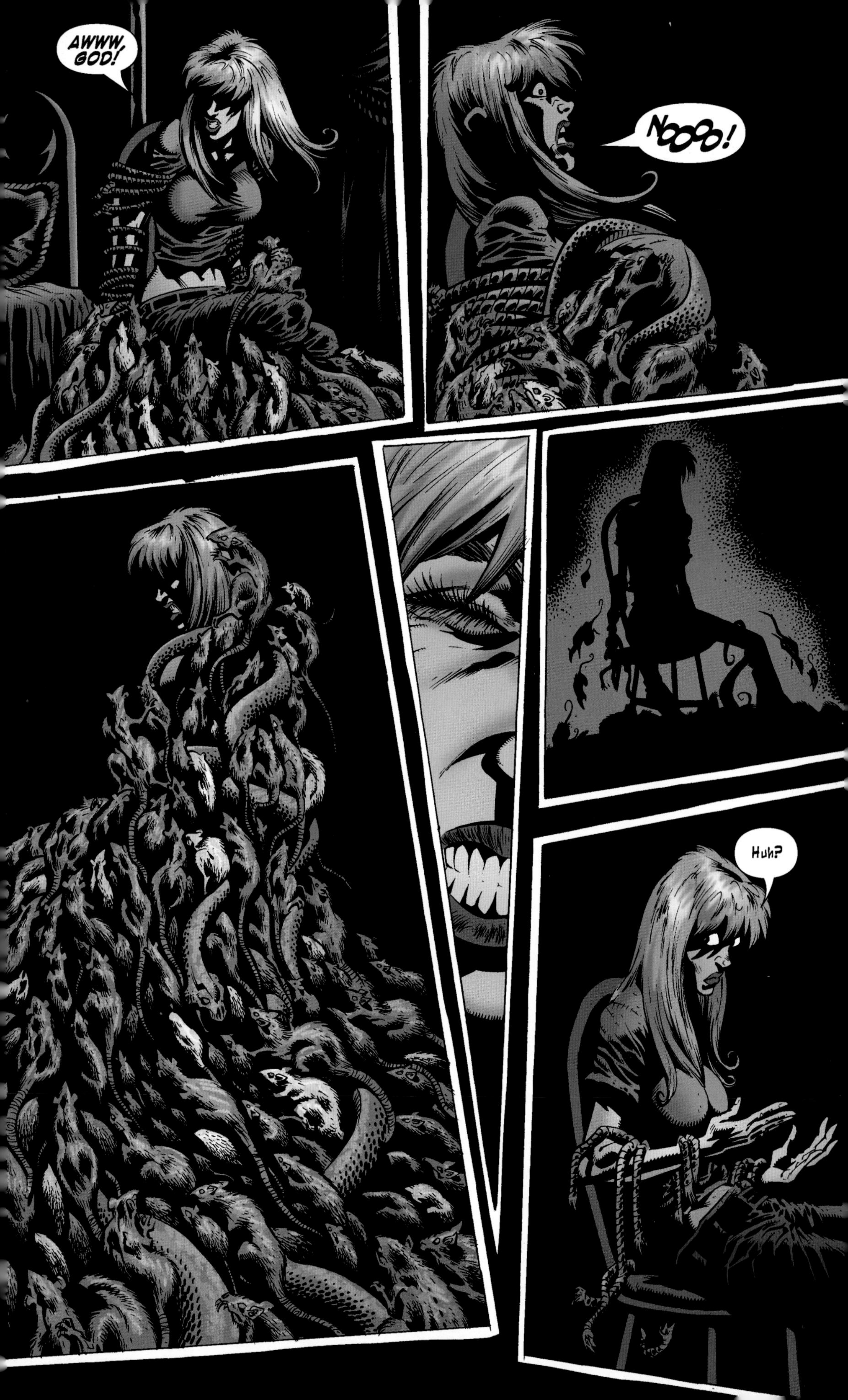
AWWW, GOD!
NOOOO!
Huh?

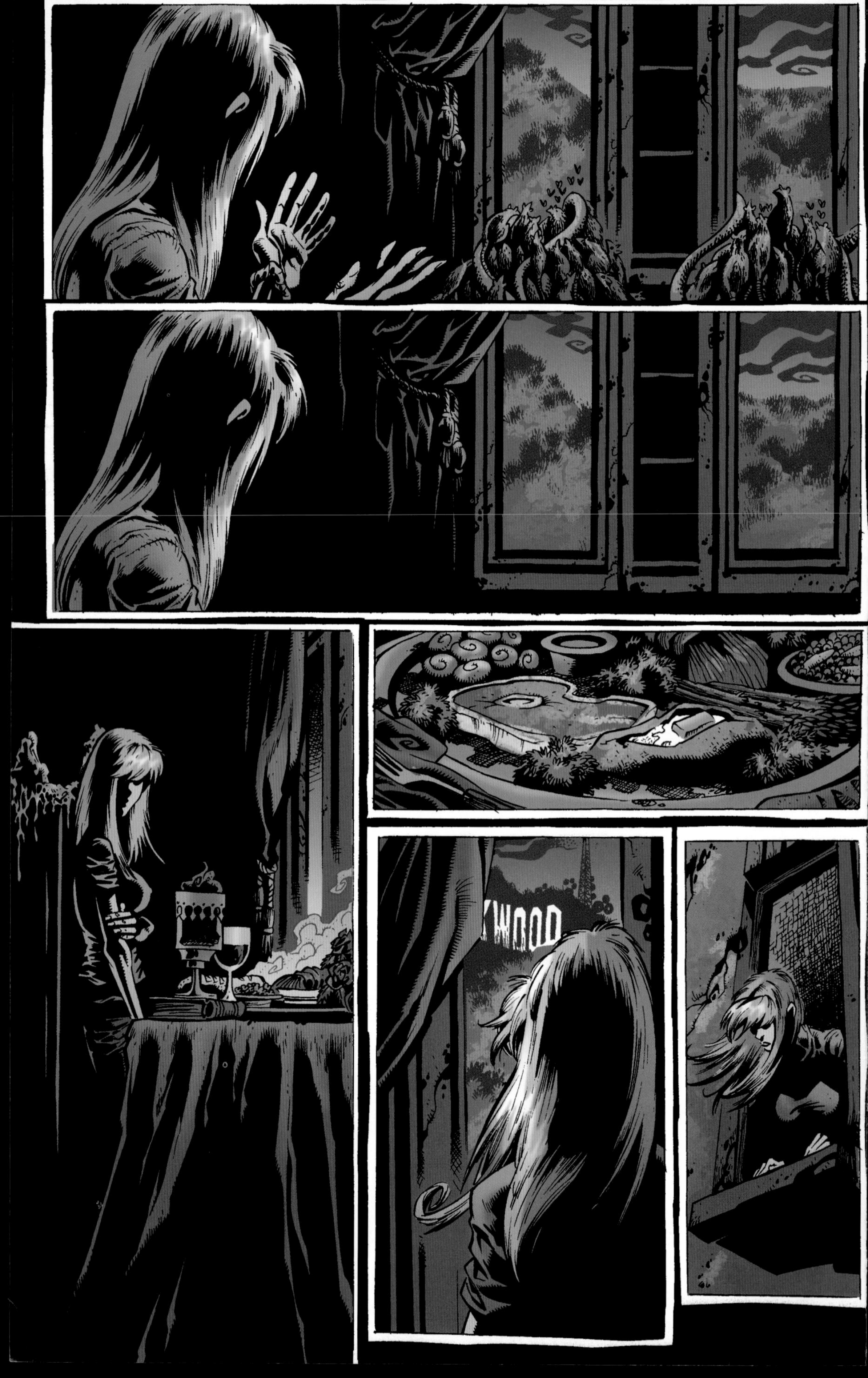
KWOOD

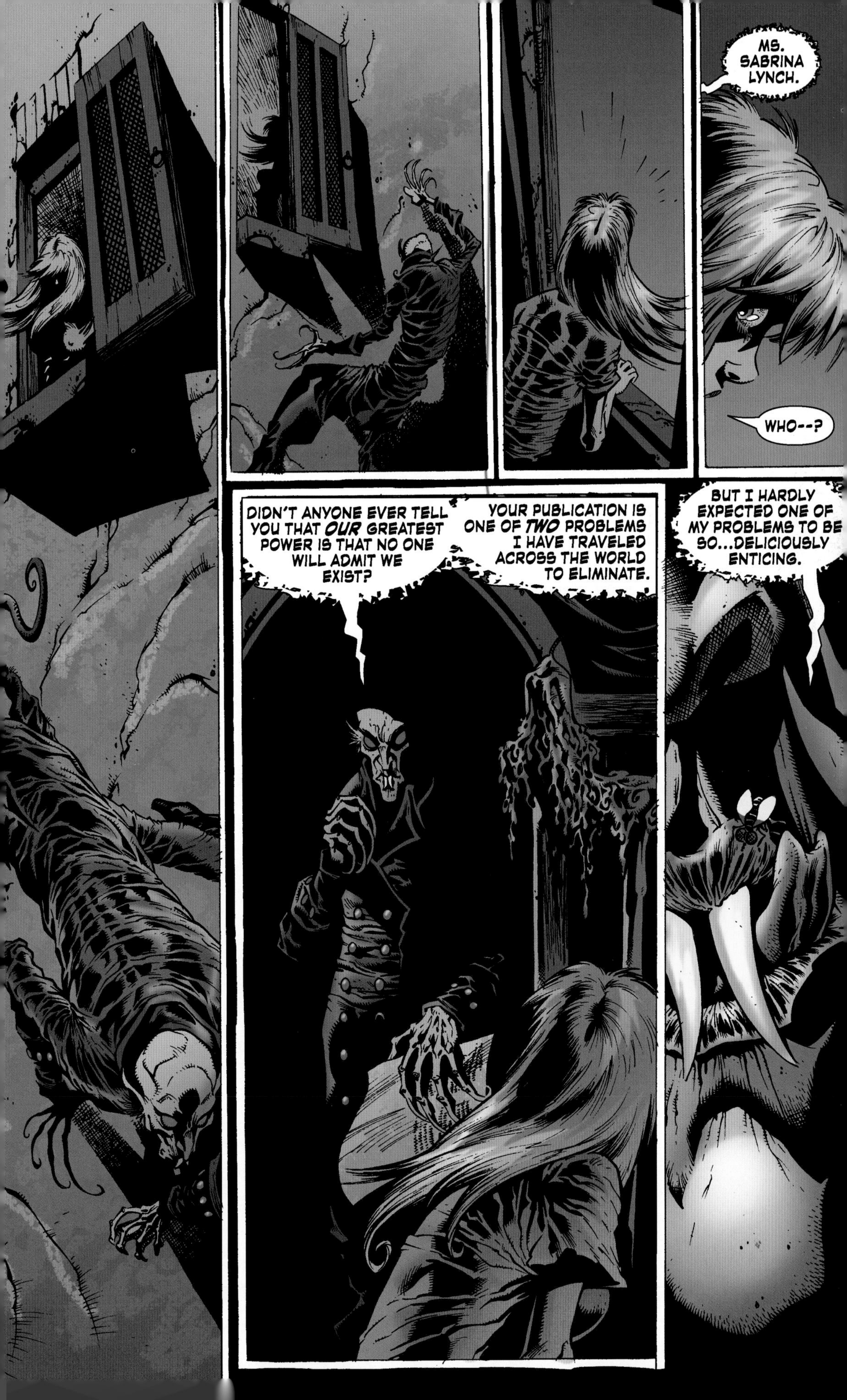
MS. SABRINA LYNCH.
WHO--?
DIDN'T ANYONE EVER TELL YOU THAT *OUR* GREATEST POWER IS THAT NO ONE WILL ADMIT WE EXIST?
YOUR PUBLICATION IS ONE OF *TWO* PROBLEMS I HAVE TRAVELED ACROSS THE WORLD TO ELIMINATE.
BUT I HARDLY EXPECTED ONE OF MY PROBLEMS TO BE SO...DELICIOUSLY ENTICING.

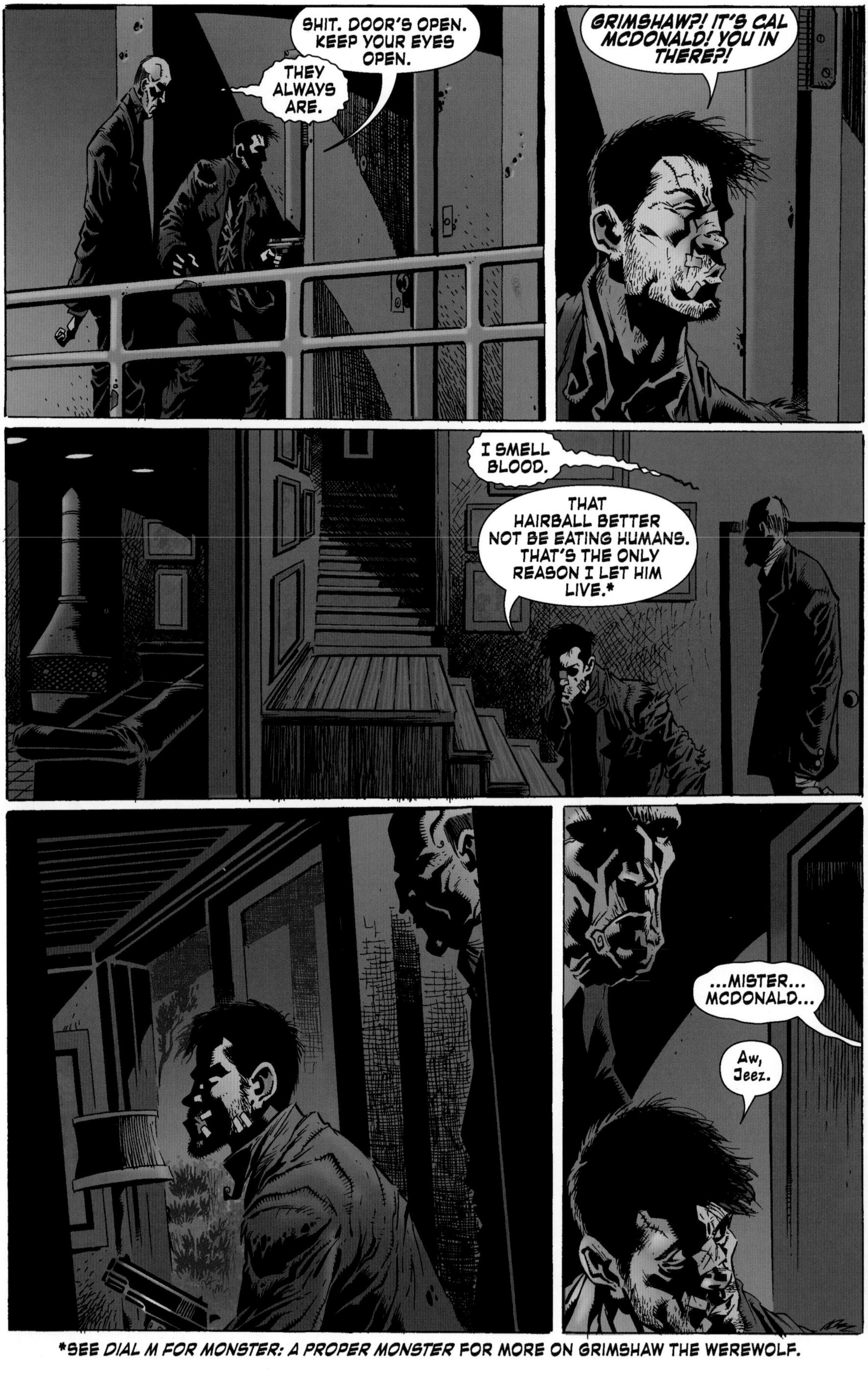
SHIT. DOOR'S OPEN. KEEP YOUR EYES OPEN.
THEY ALWAYS ARE.
GRIMSHAW?! IT'S CAL MCDONALD! YOU IN THERE?!
I SMELL BLOOD.
THAT HAIRBALL BETTER NOT BE EATING HUMANS. THAT'S THE ONLY REASON I LET HIM LIVE.*
...MISTER... MCDONALD...
Aw, Jeez.

*SEE *DIAL M FOR MONSTER: A PROPER MONSTER* FOR MORE ON GRIMSHAW THE WEREWOLF.

I'D HOPED FOR SLIGHTLY...BETTER... CIRCUMSTANCES THE NEXT TIME WE MET, MISTER M... MCDONALD.

IS THERE ANYTHING I CAN DO?

I DON'T THINK SO, BUT THANK YOU FOR OFFERING. I THINK THIS TIME I WILL NOT ESCAPE DEATH...AND TRUTHFULLY, CAL, IF I MAY CALL YOU THAT, SIR, I AM TIRED.

I HAD A GOOD LIFE. HELL, I HAD A GOOD DEATH. NOW MAYBE IT IS TIME FOR A FINAL SLEEP.

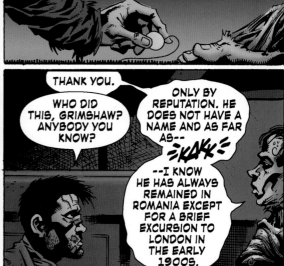

THANK YOU.

WHO DID THIS, GRIMSHAW? ANYBODY YOU KNOW?

ONLY BY REPUTATION. HE DOES NOT HAVE A NAME AND AS FAR AS--

KAK

--I KNOW HE HAS ALWAYS REMAINED IN ROMANIA EXCEPT FOR A BRIEF EXCURSION TO LONDON IN THE EARLY 1900S.

I... I'M AFRAID... I WAS NO MATCH FOR HIM. EVEN FULLY TRANSFORMED, HE GUTTED ME WITH HIS BARE HANDS.

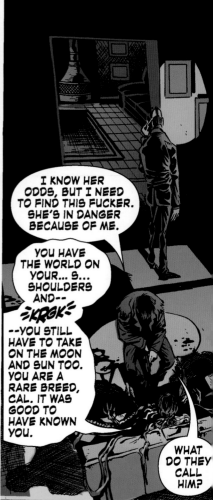

IF HE HAS HER...

HE'S GOTTA HAVE SOME SORT OF NAME. PLEASE, GRIMSHAW, HE HAS MY GIRL.

I KNOW HER ODDS, BUT I NEED TO FIND THIS FUCKER. SHE'S IN DANGER BECAUSE OF ME.

YOU HAVE THE WORLD ON YOUR... S... SHOULDERS AND--

KRGK

--YOU STILL HAVE TO TAKE ON THE MOON AND SUN TOO. YOU ARE A RARE BREED, CAL. IT WAS GOOD TO HAVE KNOWN YOU.

WHAT DO THEY CALL HIM?

NOBODY KNOWS WHO HE WAS IN LIFE, BUT IN UNDEATH, HE HAS ALWAYS BEEN CALLED...

...NOSFERATU, THE ORIGINAL UNDEAD.

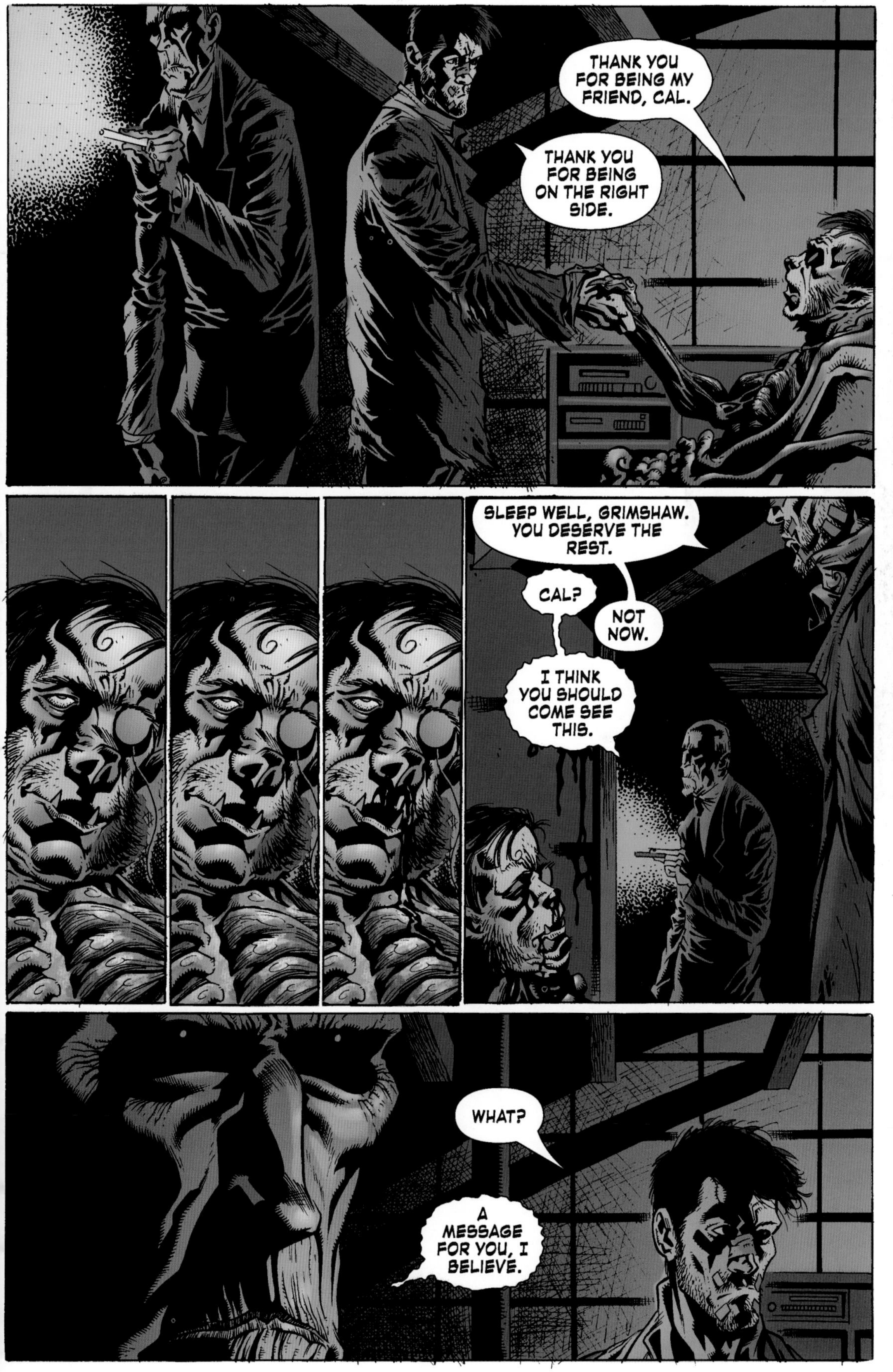
THANK YOU FOR BEING MY FRIEND, CAL.
THANK YOU FOR BEING ON THE RIGHT SIDE.
SLEEP WELL, GRIMSHAW. YOU DESERVE THE REST.
CAL?
NOT NOW.
I THINK YOU SHOULD COME SEE THIS.
WHAT?
A MESSAGE FOR YOU, I BELIEVE.

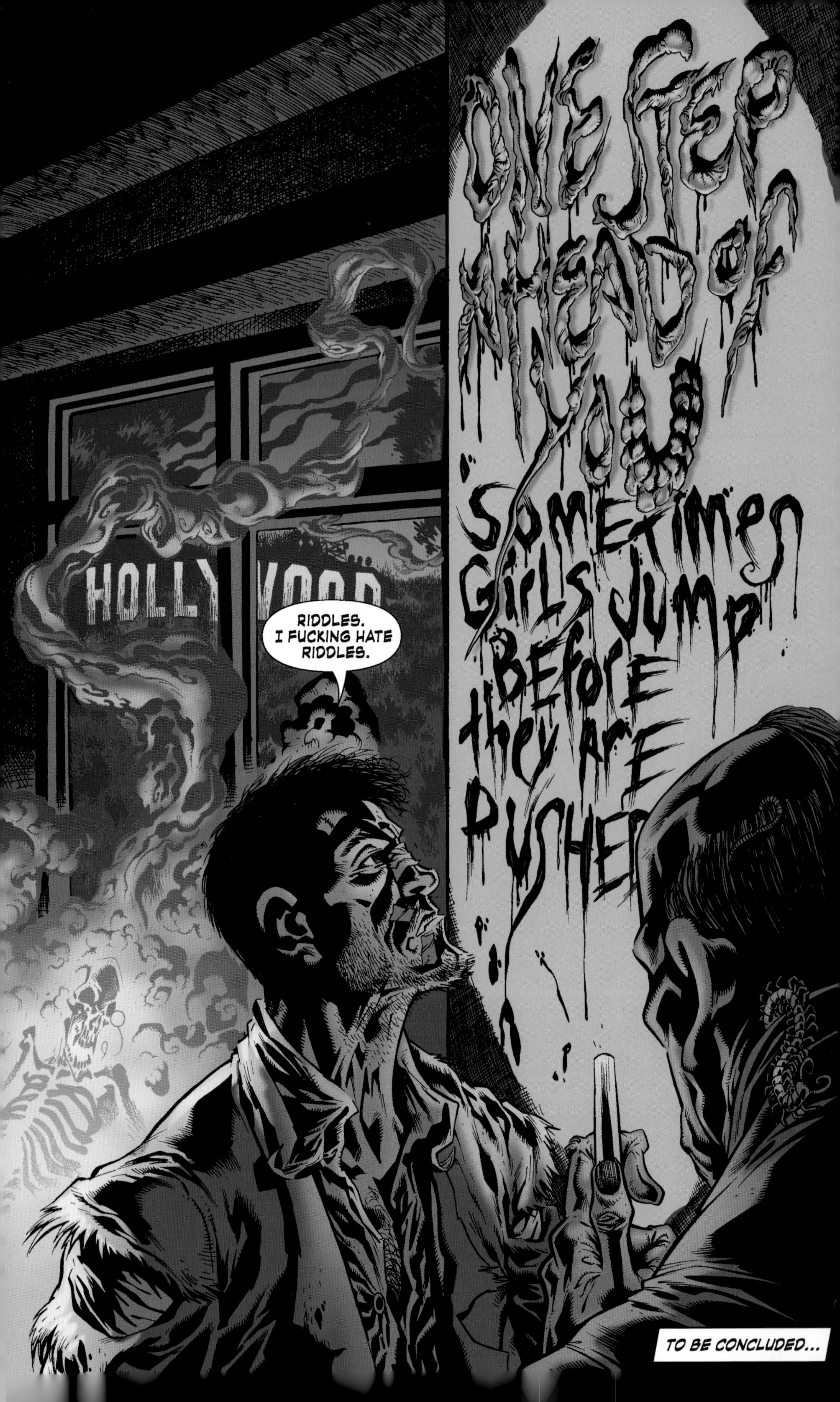
ONE STEP AHEAD OF YOU
SOMETIMES GIRLS JUMP BEFORE THEY ARE PUSHE
RIDDLES. I FUCKING HATE RIDDLES.
TO BE CONCLUDED...

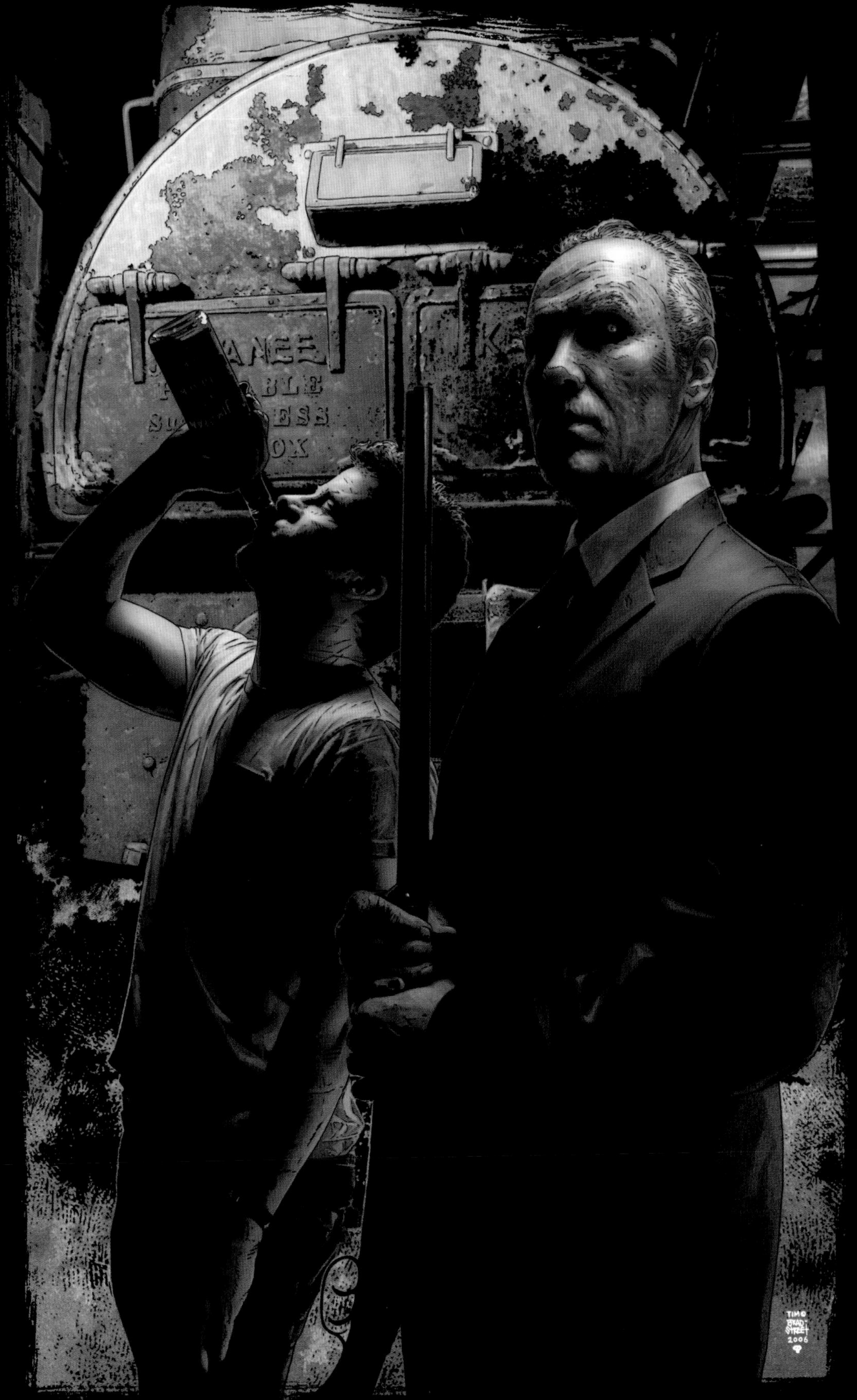

CHAPTER FOUR

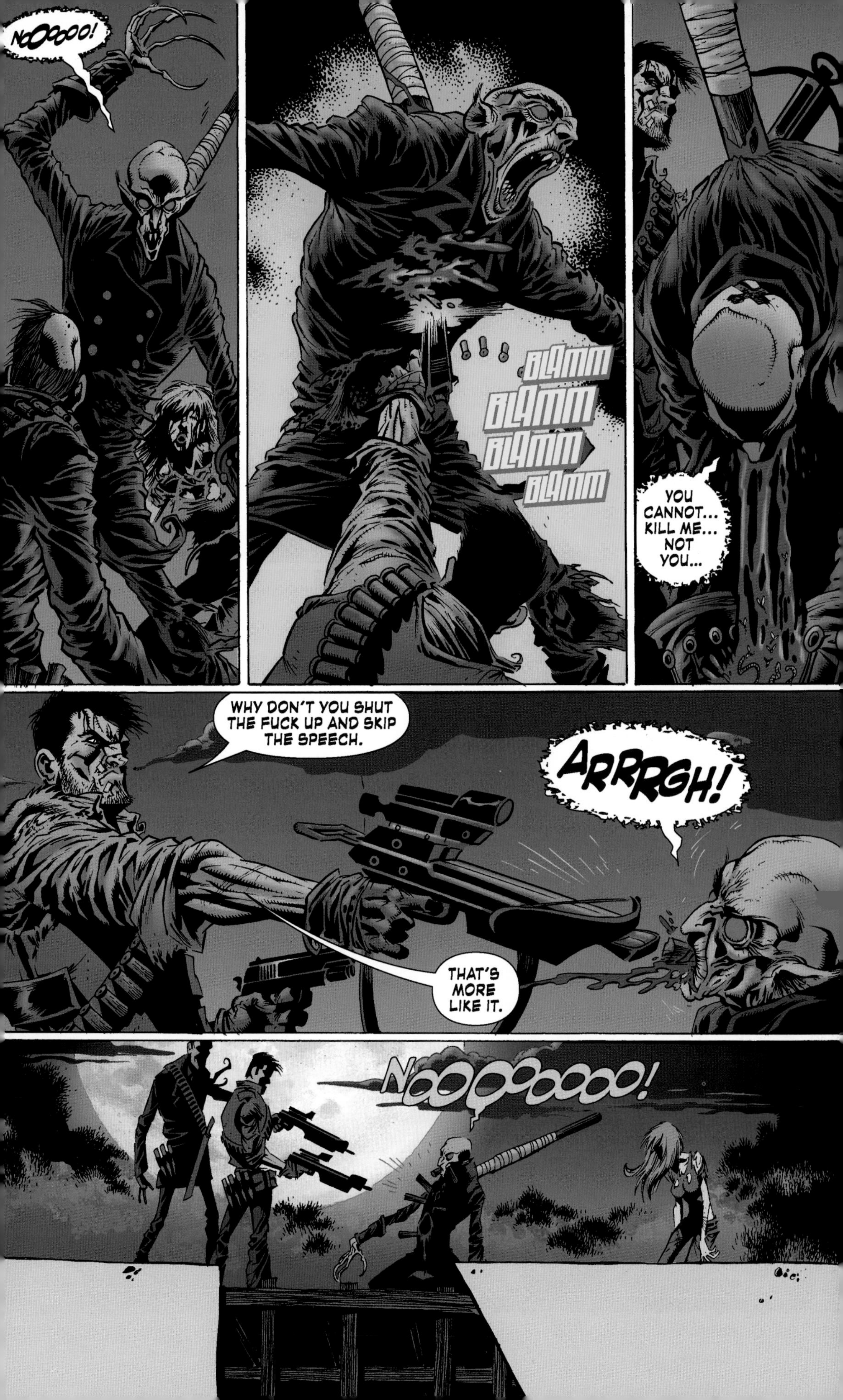
NOOOOO!
BLAMM
BLAMM
BLAMM
BLAMM
YOU CANNOT... KILL ME... NOT YOU...
WHY DON'T YOU SHUT THE FUCK UP AND SKIP THE SPEECH.
ARRRGH!
THAT'S MORE LIKE IT.
NOOOOOOOO!

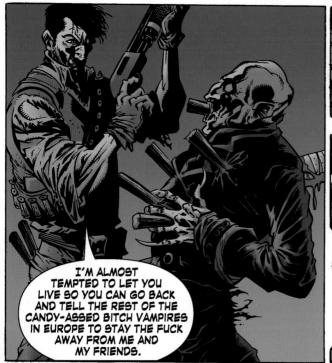

I'M ALMOST TEMPTED TO LET YOU LIVE SO YOU CAN GO BACK AND TELL THE REST OF THE CANDY-ASSED BITCH VAMPIRES IN EUROPE TO STAY THE FUCK AWAY FROM ME AND MY FRIENDS.

AHHHH!

BOOM

IT IS NOT I WHO BETRAYS THE UNDEAD.

IT IS MURDERERS LIKE YOU WHO ARE THE BETRAYERS.

GUH!

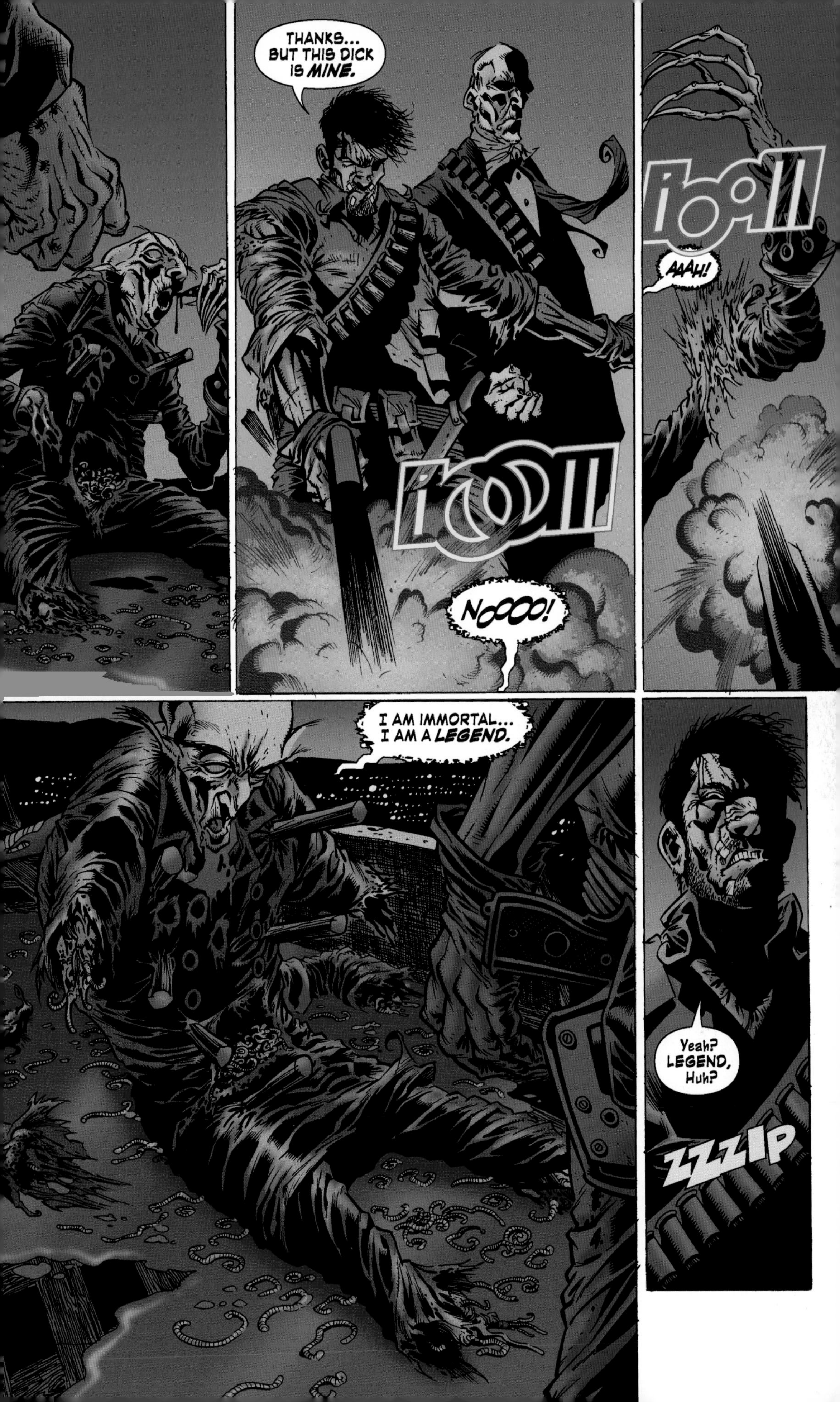

THANKS... BUT THIS DICK IS MINE.
NOOOO!
AAAH!
I AM IMMORTAL... I AM A LEGEND.
Yeah? LEGEND, Huh?
ZZZIP

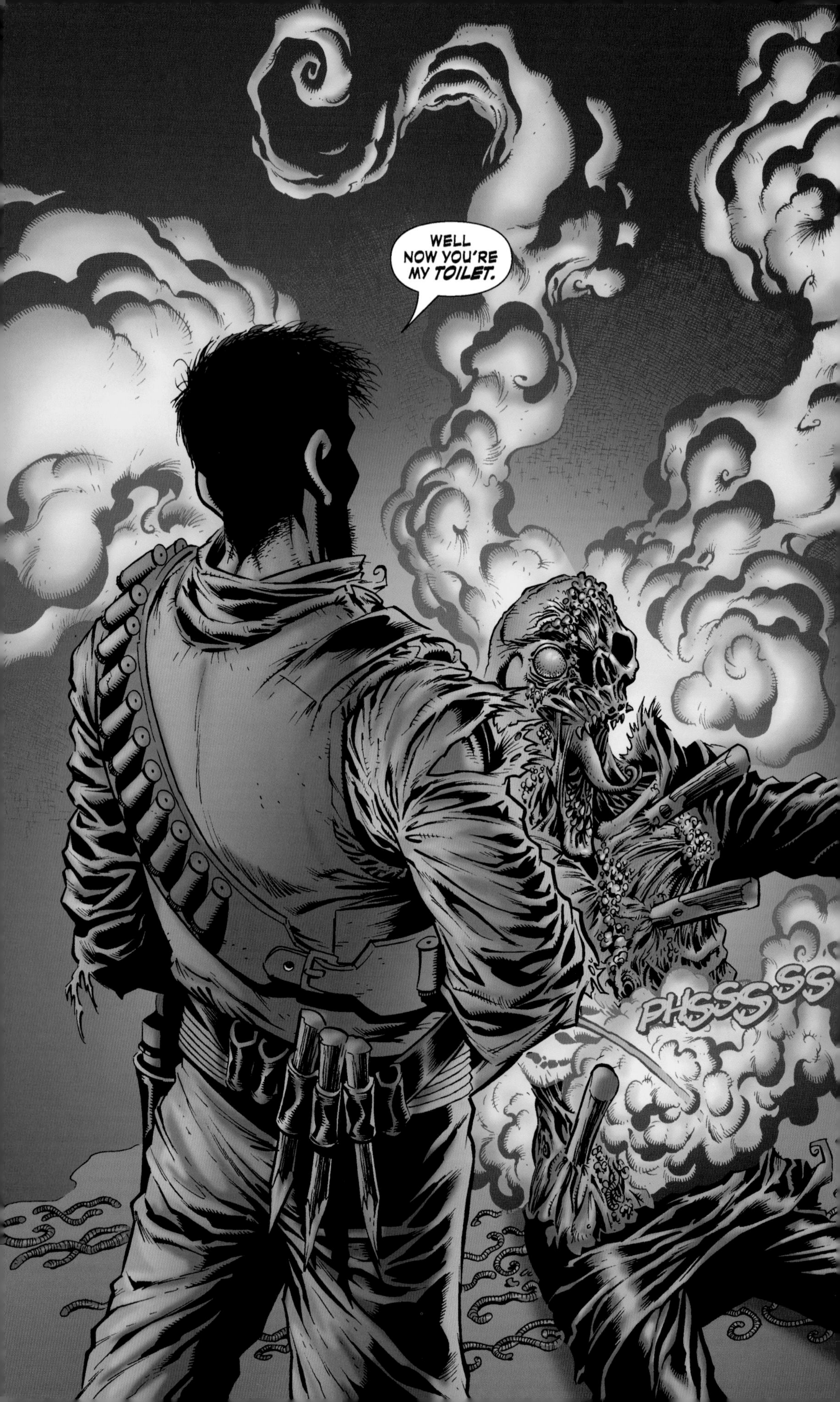
WELL NOW YOU'RE MY *TOILET.*
PHSSSSSS

ZZZIP

SABRINA.

BABE, IT'S OKAY. HE'S GONE AND--

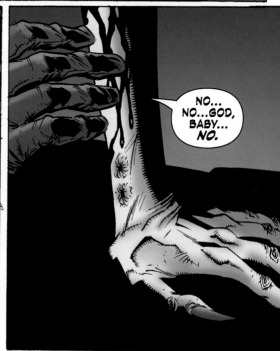

NO... NO...GOD, BABY... NO.

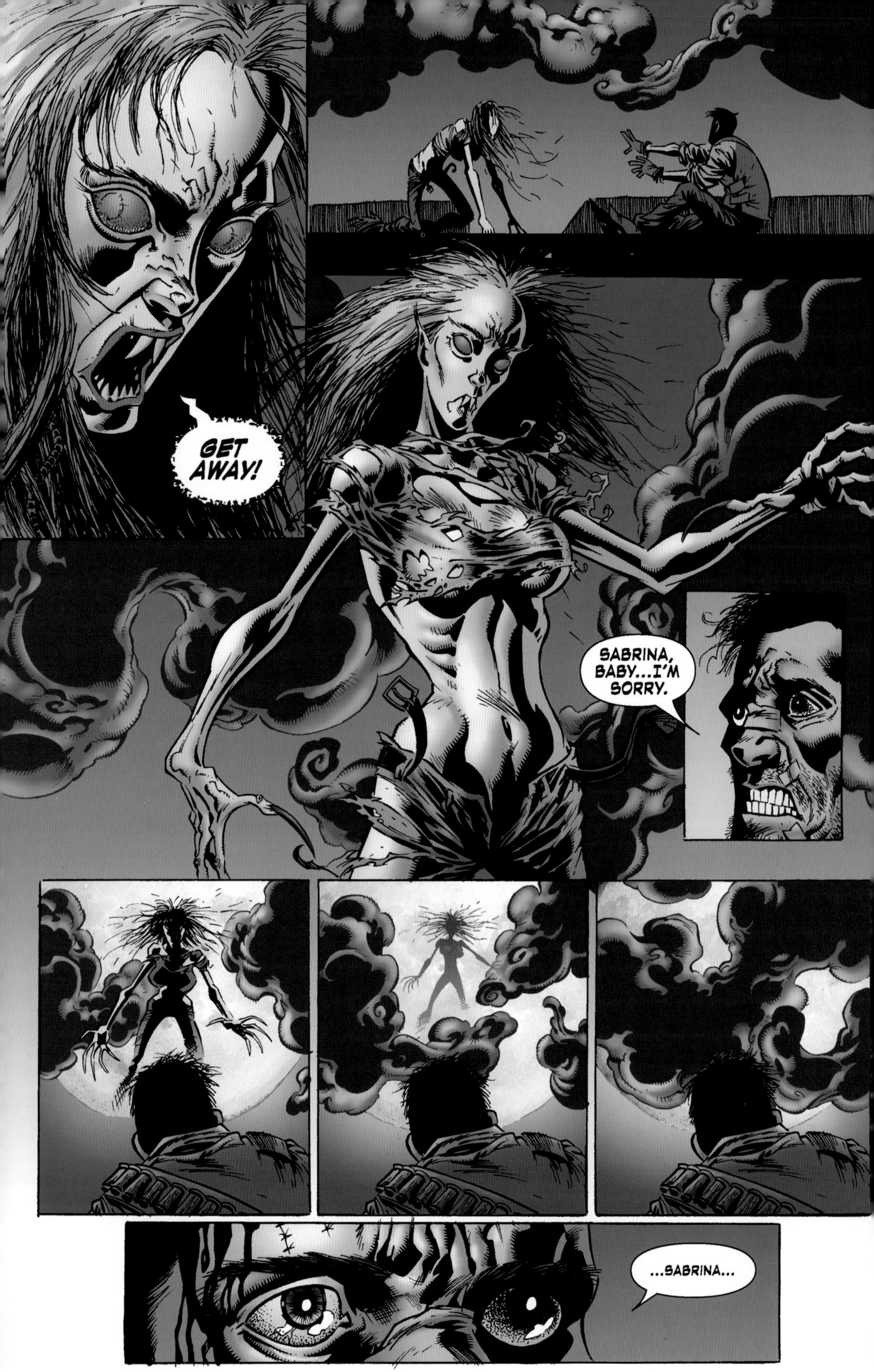
GET AWAY!
SABRINA, BABY...I'M SORRY.
...SABRINA...

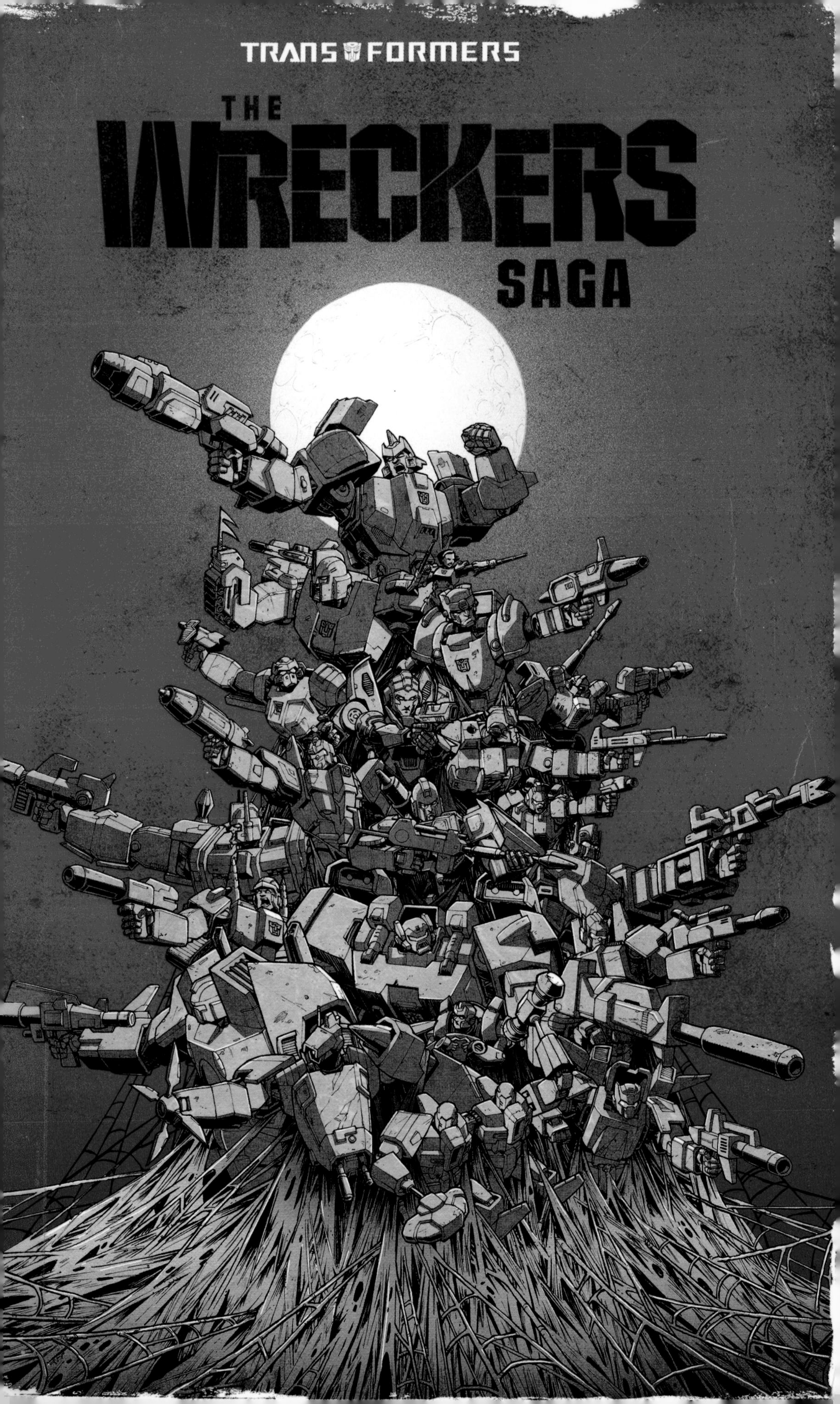
TRANSFORMERS
THE
WRECKERS
SAGA

more TRANSFORMERS from IDW:

- TRANSFORMERS WINDBLADE: THE LAST CITY
- TRANSFORMERS: AUTOCRACY TRILOGY
- TRANSFORMERS DRIFT: EMPIRES & ORIGINS
- TRANSFORMERS: REDEMPTION OF THE DINOBOTS
- TRANSFORMERS: IDW COLLECTON PHASE TWO, VOL. 1-7